Edward Yang |

Contemporary Film Directors

Edited by James Naremore

The Contemporary Film Directors series provides concise, well-written introductions to directors from around the world and from every level of the film industry. Its chief aims are to broaden our awareness of important artists, to give serious critical attention to their work, and to illustrate the variety and vitality of contemporary cinema. Contributors to the series include an array of internationally respected critics and academics. Each volume contains an incisive critical commentary, an informative interview with the director, and a detailed filmography.

A list of books in the series appears
at the end of this book.

Edward Yang |

John Anderson

UNIVERSITY
OF
ILLINOIS
PRESS
URBANA
AND
CHICAGO

♾ This book is printed on acid-free paper.

Library of Congress Cataloging-in-Publication Data
Anderson, John, 1955 March 10–
Edward Yang / John Anderson.
p. cm. — (Contemporary film directors)
Filmography: p.
Includes bibliographical references and index.
ISBN 0-252-02993-3 (alk. paper)
ISBN 0-252-07236-7 (pbk. : alk. paper)
1. Yang, Dechang, 1947—Criticism and interpretation.
I. Title. II. Series.
PN1998.3.Y38A53   2005
791.4302'33'092—dc22   2004020464

Frontispiece: Edward Yang after the awards ceremony
at the Cannes Film Festival, 2000

Contents |

Preface and Acknowledgments | ix

POETRY AND MOTION | 1

Expectations 20

That Day, on the Beach 26

Taipei Story 34

The Terrorizer 45

A Brighter Summer Day 54

A Confucian Confusion 66

Mahjong 77

Yi Yi 84

AN INTERVIEW WITH EDWARD YANG | 95

Filmography | 117

Bibliography | 123

Index | 125

A startling example of free association, someone wrily called it later on that rainy New York afternoon. But how could he know? Remembered now, the moment seems to have been more of a coalescence of existing certainties, vague intellectual suspicions, and redolent emotions. The kind of thing that could have amounted to an obvious critical synthesis for someone else, it was a small epiphany for me.

The question to us panelists—seated during a conference on Asian cinema at Columbia University—was about our most memorable moment during an Asian film. The critic Dave Kehr recalled the first time he saw a work by Hou Hsiao-hsien; someone else (Lisa Schwartzbaum? Amy Taubin, maybe?) reminisced about some hallucinatory martial-arts moment. All that came to my mind, however, was my experience watching Edward Yang's epic *A Brighter Summer Day* and how the conflicts among its characters—about place, identity, immigration, violence, and borrowed culture—had mirrored the American experience, while at the same time being specifically Taiwanese. This subtle collision of cultures said so much, so eloquently, about the universal potential of film and the universality of Yang.

There is probably little need to elaborate on how seldom that potential is realized in films nor any need to reconstruct here what I said that day at Columbia. What's important is to understand that Yang, like every great artist, transcends both the place and the time in which his best work is situated, becoming a guideline (in the Alpine sense of the word) to people on every side of the mountain.

This book is written strictly from an American viewpoint; I am not Asian, nor can I claim particular scholarship in Asian cinema. But in approaching the work of Edward Yang, I think this may be an asset.

Yang has spent so much time in the United States, and his work is so expressively informed by America, its culture, and its cultural detritus, that it is just as important for a viewer to recognize the semiotic importance and imperial resonance of a Yankees baseball cap as it is to know that the "three ways" of Chinese thought are Taoism, Buddhism, and Confucianism.

Among the people I would like to acknowledge for their help in the preparation of this book are Kent Jones, Richard Pena, Norman Wang, Wendy Liddell, Stuart Klawans, James Naremore, Joan Catapano (for holding my feet gently to the fire), and, of course, Edward Yang, one of the loveliest men and gentlest souls one would ever have the good fortune to meet. His generosity with his time and his mind, be it in person or in his often voluminous but always passionate e-mail responses to my questions, has been inspiring. (Unless otherwise attributed, quotations from Yang in this book are from these exchanges, which took place in late 2002.)

On a more highly personal note, I'd like to thank my daughters, Kellye, Maureen, and Sophie, for their love, and Diane Weyermann, for everything she granted me.

Edward Yang |

Poetry and Motion |

In his introduction to an anthology of British verse, published in the 1960s, the influential and innovative W. H. Auden suggested criteria for recognizing a "major" poet. There must be:

1. A large body of work;
2. A wide range of subject matter and treatment;
3. An unmistakable originality of vision and style;
4. A mastery of technique;
5. A constant, progressive process of maturation—the point of which being that, should an author's individual works be placed side by side at any stage of his or her career, it would always be clear which work came first and which came after.

What the work of Edward Yang proves of Auden's strictures is that certain formulas are worth only so much. Yang is a poet of film, a director less interested perhaps in pure image than in ideas, a director whose work is often so sophisticated in its thinking that it should be accompanied by footnotes. Nevertheless . . .

Thankfully, Auden offered no rules regarding celebrity versus obscurity, and how could he? Poetry has never, even in any earlier age, enjoyed the popularity we would like to think it had—because if it had, we'd be better people than we are and less in need of poetry.

Similarly, art cinema, having more or less the same popular status as fine literature and thus being the poetry of the new millennium (and its increasingly image-driven culture), enjoys more people talking about it than watching it. Given that Taiwan's cinema is inseparable from its literature, and given that Edward Yang is the most novelistic of Taiwan's small but potent catalog of world-class filmmakers (because of his insistence on narrative structure, interconnections, and even the occasional resolution), we might be excused for applying to him Auden's rules of greatness, especially since, as Auden himself also suggested, only three and a half of the five rules need be met.

Rule No. 1: Sorry, no. Although a founding father of the Taiwanese New Wave, which erupted with monsoon-like ferocity against complacent, conventional native filmmaking at the beginning of the 1980s, Yang has not had the most prolific of careers. He has produced only seven films of feature length since 1983. (However, all of his features run from a minimum of two hours to as much as four hours, which would make Yang's screentime the equivalent of one and a half times that of most other directors.)

Rule No. 2: Again, no. Yang's predominating landscape, although not his only one, has been Taiwan itself—and, more specifically, the capital, Taipei. It is hard to think of any major creative artist who can so comfortably be placed beside the likes of Joyce, Vermeer, or even Woody Allen as someone whose work is so inescapably linked with a specific city—even if that work elegantly transcends its place of origin to embrace themes and emotions that supersede geography and even culture.

Otherwise, Yang is a major filmmaker—and filmmaking poet—by anyone's standards. His talents as a visual storyteller, which are rooted in his teenage fascination and prize-winning work with manga, or Japanese-style comic-book art, and his facility with the medium have been apparent since his earliest films. *The Terrorizer,* which dates from 1986, is comparable in form, function, and philosophy to the mature work of Claude Chabrol in its psychological insightfulness and mastery of form.

Yang has been compared early and often in his career with Michelangelo Antonioni. The critic Jonathan Rosenbaum has written of Yang's *Taipei Story:*

> Much as *The Terrorizer* evokes the chance encounters and ambiguous photographic images of Antonioni's *Blowup,* this film about the interrelated perils of love and capitalism is periodically reminiscent of Antonioni's *Eclipse:* the places occupied and unoccupied feel similarly haunted, and a constellation of characters both older and younger than the two leads extends the sense of malaise to other generations. Unfortunately this brief description makes *Taipei Story* sound more schematic and less poetic than it is; the moods it conjures up are potent and indelible.

"Maybe Italian neo-realism affected us," Yang has said, "because its methods looked so inexpensive, and we had no money" (Interview 130).

Yang has, arguably, exhibited a far wider field of vision and a more humanistic (maybe even grudgingly optimistic) worldview than have his Italian predecessor or most leading filmmakers, Eastern or Western. His work is a marriage of omnipotent observation and heartfelt empathy with characters who may be flawed, or foolish, but are never to be abandoned. We can easily embrace even the most callow of his characters, drawn as they are from the ever-evolving zeitgeist Yang chronicles in his occasionally fantasy-embellished but essentially reality-based films.

The "process" of Edward Yang, the evolution of the man as an artist, moral observer, and social critic, has been as fascinating to watch as most of his movies. *Yi Yi,* his masterpiece of 2000 and his first film to get a wide release in the United States, provided a sense of validation among his worldwide supporters. His earnestness may never have been in doubt, but he seemed better able, suddenly, to access his best instincts.

As a result, he has attracted previously unwon worldwide attention. "I am reminded, oddly but truly," the critic John Leonard said while reviewing *Yi Yi* on CBS television, "of the stories of John Cheever, which spoke of simplicity and usefulness; of stamina, valor, virtue, kindness and beauty; of what he called 'that sense of sanctuary that is the essence of love'; and of the shadow that falls on all of these."

Yang's view of his own work has been far more restrained. "I tried to get everything as average as possible," he said with characteristic understatement, not long after the film had played the 2000 Cannes Film Festival and he was awarded the prize for Best Director. "Not too much, not too little, right down the center of the court, because that's what is most universal. It will touch more people that way. And, actually, it's more dramatic" (qtd. in Johnston).

"When you make a film like this," he told another interviewer, "it's like writing a very intimate letter to a very good friend. The movie's success is not something that boosts my ego. But that there are so many friends in the world who understand you—that's a comfortable feeling" (qtd. in Johnston).

Comfortable for Yang, perhaps, but the overarching effect of his films is as far from solace as the feel-good ethos of current Hollywood is from the blunt-edged humanity of Jean Renoir. All of Yang's films are disquieting, albeit in their own distinct ways. The silent solitude of *Expectations* (1982), the spiritual slipperiness of *That Day, on the Beach* (1983), the existential dread of *The Terrorizer* (1986), and the interpersonal dysfunction of *A Confucian Confusion* (1994) and *Mahjong* (1996) are all intended to rock audiences out of their popcorn-nourished complacency and into a new awareness of their world and its possibilities.

These films are not the stuff of record-shattering box office, nor have they had global exposure, as one can tell from Yang's record with U.S. distributors. But mass acceptance has never been a barometer of artistic importance. It certainly has not been in the case of Edward Yang.

That his films have had trouble even in Taiwan is an example of what happens to agents provocateurs on the field of mass entertainment. The principals of the Taiwanese New Wave were, of course, Asian filmmakers, who were influenced by the Italian neo-realists—who inspired the realism that separates the younger Taiwanese directors from their predecessors—and impelled not only by artistic hunger but by a need to explore the singular experience of life on Taiwan. With his contribution to the portmanteau *In Our Time* (1982), his debut feature, *That Day, on the Beach,* and his landmark *Taipei Story* (1985), Yang presented modern Taiwanese audiences with something they had not been shown: themselves; real, recognizable, everyday people, framed by the particular strangeness and complexity of life on their island.

With the propulsively dramatic, psychologically ruinous *A Brighter Summer Day* (1991), Yang's vision crystallized, as he showed how Taiwan's schizophrenia could be translated into a medium that both revealed and healed. Yang bookended the nineties with *A Brighter Summer Day* and *Yi Yi*, achieving with the latter film a kind of synthesis of his own disparate tensions and the full realization of his Tolstoy-esque talents as a storyteller. But Yang spent most of the decade making movies that were more respectable than revelatory. All the same, during this period, while mounting several stage plays, he attempted to create a kind of soul portrait of Taipei.

The patchwork culture of Taiwanese society, its lack of a traditionally solid foundation, and its seduction by the economic bull markets of the nineties have been consistent themes for Yang over the last decade. *A Confucian Confusion* (1994) is an aptly titled omnibus of unhappy characters romantically involved with the wrong people for the wrong reasons, mostly money, which Yang sees as Taipei's chief pollutant and major religion. A messy black comedy of ill-manners and spiritual distress, the film was made before Asia's mid-decade economic meltdown, when Taiwan's wealth was as rampant as its apparent paranoia. *Mahjong* (1996) was similarly obsessed with the materialism of Taipei, the city's lure as a quick-money magnet, and the soullessness that infects any place obsessed with gain for gain's sake. These two films are often seen, thematically, as a pair, just as Yang's "urban trilogy" (*That Day, on the Beach; Taipei Story;* and *The Terrorizer*) serves as a medley of alienation. Similarly, the noncontiguous *Yi Yi* and *A Brighter Summer Day* are joined by themes and structure. A bit ironically, perhaps, *Confucian Confusion* and *Mahjong* are the easiest to cite as concrete examples of Yang's love-hate relationship with the city of his childhood.

Born in Shanghai in 1947, Yang was taken to Taiwan by his family in 1949, after Mao Zedong took over the mainland and the Nationalists hit the rowboats. Growing up in the fifties and sixties, he was among his country's first postwar generation and thus a product of a society (and a government-encouraged ethos) that stressed the study of science and math to the exclusion of the arts—at least as a pursuit for respectable people

"I used to enjoy drawing comics when I was a kid," Yang once said, but as he explains in an interview elsewhere in this book, cultural matters or, for that matter, "anything that improves people's intelligence," was denigrated on Taiwan. Young people who could find the strength to resist the status quo and follow an artistic path were few, and they had to have been particularly courageous.

The young Edward Yang was not. As he freely admits, Yang "gave in," forsaking his first career choice, architecture—which he had imagined as a discipline that could reconcile the creative with the technical—and opting instead for a degree in electrical engineering. (He was compelled, he has said, to be "a good Chinese son.") This led to a move to the United States, where he received a master's degree in computer design at the University of Florida, after which he went west, enrolling for just a year in the film program at the University of Southern California. ("It was a disastrous experience: I couldn't do a lot of the things they wanted me to do. My ideas about story and characters were so different.")

After dropping out, he spent seven years in Washington state, from 1974 to 1981. "I found a job in Seattle designing computers [at the University of Washington], and started working from eight to five. By the time I was thirty, I felt so old. Then one day I passed a cinema with a sign saying *Aguirre, the Wrath of God.* I walked in and came out a different person."

Aguirre, one of Werner Herzog's famously mad exercises in excess (other notorious examples are *Fitzcarraldo* and *Nosferatu,* all three starring Klaus Kinski), is about an insane conquistador in search of gold in the Incan Amazon. "Basically it's not the style or the beauty of the images that influenced me," Yang recalled, tellingly. "It was the spirit of the filmmaking of Mr. Herzog that was never before seen."

Deciding, on a wave of Herzog/Kinski–inspired determination that "I had to do something I liked before I got real old," Yang returned to Taiwan in 1981 to pursue a filmmaking career. (Another German, Rainer Werner Fassbinder, has been cited as a motivating force as well.)

"The actual New Wave arrived exactly at the moment when the Nationalist regime was overtaken by crisis," Yang told the *New Left Review* in 2001.

> That was in 1979, when Carter established diplomatic relations with mainland China, dropping the KMT into limbo. Losing its seat in the UN, which happened in 1973, was bad enough. But losing its privileged

Edward Yang met Werner Herzog for the first time
at the San Francisco International Film Festival,
April 1995. (All photos courtesy of Edward Yang)

connection to the U.S. was a much worse shock. The regime suddenly
looked quite isolated—it was the low point in its political fortunes.
People in Taiwan were thoroughly disillusioned with its propaganda,
and now much more confident in confronting it.

After big demonstrations, the government finally lifted martial law,
which had been in force ever since 1949. There was no democracy yet,
but political controls weakened, and culturally it became more possible
to defy the censor.

I had been in the States for a decade after graduating in Taipei—
studying in Florida and LA and then working in a computer company
in Seattle. When I saw what was happening, I decided to head back and
make some films. I was then 33. ("Taiwan Stories" 131)

Yang's first job was for a friend, Yu Weizeng, a director he had met
at USC and for whom he would write and produce *The Winter of 1905*.
This was followed by his first work as a writer-director, *Floating Weeds*,
a TV two-parter. He may have left the United States, but a vapor trail
of Americana—Yankee caps, rock 'n' roll, exported boorishness—has
drifted through his work ever since.

In 1988, Yang told a different tale of his artistic epiphany to an American journalist, who related it thusly:

> When William Holden rode across the screen in the 1953 American Western *Escape from Fort Bravo*, he didn't know his performance would help launch Taiwan's "new wave" of filmmakers more than 25 years later.
>
> But sitting in a dark Taipei theater in the early 1950s was a 6-year-old Chinese boy. He couldn't take his eyes off of the good looks and charismatic ways of Holden.
>
> That little boy today recalls the "cowboys, cavalry, pretty girls, circling the wagons, having to fight their way out—it was a lot of fun. It was the excitement that you don't see in everyday life. I went to school the next day and was telling all my classmates about the story for so long that I lost my voice." (qtd. in Babcock 19)

During the period when Taiwan's New Wave was germinating, Yang has recalled, the fledgling filmmakers who would eventually found that 1980s movement—including Yang's only rival among Taiwanese directors, Hou Hsiao-hsien—would hang out at Yang's house, which lacked even a lock on the door (since "there was nothing to steal").

The house at 69 Tsinan Road, Taipei, where
everything happened for Taiwan New Wave cinema.

"All these guys would just gather in my house, talking and laughing and drinking: Hou Hsiao-hsien, Wu Nianzhen—just about all of them," Yang said. "You could just push open the door. Everyone just wanted to do similar things. We weren't allowed to, and no one was willing to give us any money to, but we shared all these idealistic thoughts" (qtd. in Kraicer and Roosen-Runge).

It is a scenario that suggests Hawthorne and Melville, hanging out and getting metaphysical in the Berkshires; Dizzy Gillespie and Charlie Parker, hanging out and rearranging the history of jazz; Burroughs, Ginsberg, and Kerouac, hanging out and smoking dope in the dorm rooms of Columbia—a serendipitous tryst of geniuses, each of whom would eventually have an impact on his art form, one way or the other, and whose mutual influences are evident and enormous. In 1985, the same year he made the essential *A Time to Live and a Time to Die,* Hou gave a startling performance as a disillusioned baseball player in Yang's *Taipei Story,* a film that, as has often been said, helped to change the face of Taiwanese cinema.

As dramatically as Taiwanese cinema has changed, so have world cinema and the dynamics at play between movie markets. To Yang, U.S. distribution is not all that important: "There's enough demand for good local films from Taiwan, Hong Kong, Korea and Japan that the Japanese investors in the project will make money in Asia without having to depend on the U.S. market. So the film can be long, almost three hours long, and it can tell a story without car chases or special effects and it can deal with the politics of Taiwan without having to explain everything to audiences, who might even know what the title means."

It is paradoxical, then, that *Yi Yi* has yet to be released in its country of origin. But even though 98 percent of the films released in Taiwan are American, Yang has professed no desire to work elsewhere. "I can do a lot of things which I wouldn't be allowed in Hollywood," he once said, "like produce my own movies and work with new actors." He insists he does not feel isolated:

Our environment is no longer determined by geography. And a lot of big cities are growing more and more similar. You watch TV, you call a cab, you go to the office and turn on your computer, read your e-mail and surf Web sites all over the world. When you go out, someone phones you on your mobile from Hong Kong. I look at globalization in a positive way, not in terms of there being a McDonald's or Starbucks everywhere. We are beginning to realize we have more in common than that. And that makes the diversity and subtle differences between us even more interesting.

Yang formed his own production company, Yang and His Gang, in 1989. (It was renamed Atom Films and Theater in 1992 and expanded to include stage work. In addition to financing and producing films and plays, the company is involved in experimental high-tech multimedia work.) But he waited fifteen years to make *Yi Yi*, having been inspired by a friend's father's coma. (In the film, the grandmother is in a coma as the result of a stroke.)

Only in 1999, he said, did he feel he had developed the maturity to tackle such a sweeping, three-hour Taiwanese family drama. ("To describe it as a three-hour Taiwanese family drama," wrote Nigel Andrews, in the *Financial Times* of London, "is like calling 'Citizen Kane' a film about a newspaper.")

"I don't usually talk about my films," Yang once said, relating a tale about one film festival's organizers, who polled their participants about why they made films. "I put it very simply," he said. "'So I don't have to speak so much.'"

But he does occasionally speak. "My former schoolmates are all billionaires in Taiwan," he has said. "I was the first to cross the border from technology [to art], so half my time is spent speaking to staff [at high-tech corporations] to keep them aware of the humanity side."

All he would need to do, it seems, is show them his films.

Yangst

> The bombs we plant in each other are ticking away.
>
> —Edward Yang

With 609 people per square kilometer, Taiwan is one of the most densely populated places on earth. Despite having more than 22 million people, it can evidently boast one of the highest concentrations of genius of any location on the planet (compare, if you will, early twentieth-century Ireland and its literature to early twenty-first-century Taiwan and its cinema).

It is also the only place in China to have legitimately, democratically elected a government, although this did not happen until 1999, when the long-governing Kuomintang was replaced peacefully. This was a first in the history of Taiwan, a place with a bloody, violent past. In 1947, for example, there was an uprising that the Nationalists from the mainland—who had chased the Japanese out of Taiwan but then treated the place like a possession—put down with brutal force. Twenty thousand natives were slaughtered in what would be known as the "February 28 incident"—a euphemism also used later by mainland Chinese to describe what happened at Tiananmen Square.

The 1947 massacre and subsequent decades of Leninist-derived Kuomintang rule created animosity between native and emigré, fostering an unavoidably hostile atmosphere of the type portrayed in *A Brighter Summer Day.* Yang was raised amid the conflicted milieu he depicts in that film, a place where the younger generation grows up hearing the only home they have ever known insulted consistently by the people who brought them there. That the kids turn a deaf ear to their elders while being drawn to the borrowed culture of the West—and to the samurai swords left behind by the departed Japanese—is not particularly surprising.

If Yang's *Taipei Story* changed the face of Taiwanese cinema, it was a face that needed changing. Before the New Wave, movies in Taiwan were a curious (as in corrupt) business, as most business there seems to be, if the picture painted in films such as *Mahjong,* Yang's go-go 1990s comedy, is even remotely accurate. But the corruption itself was a catalyst for the new filmmakers, enabling Yang and his colleagues to make their first features.

There are three Chinese cinemas, those of Hong Kong, Taiwan, and the mainland, and they are all rooted in the Shanghai cinema of the 1920s and 1930s. By the late 1970s, however, the three industries had become quite distinct.

Hong Kong cinema, which often used Taiwan as a backlot (for its spectacular scenery), was booming. The Shaw Brothers studio was churning out features by directors who had honed the Mandarin sword-play epic to a fine edge. Through the historical film and other genre pictures, the Shaw empire had reached the pinnacle of its power, making films that were shown all over Southeast Asia and in Chinatowns across the globe.

Golden Harvest and its biggest star, Bruce Lee, were also on the rise. Interaction and cooperation between the film industries in Hong Kong and Taiwan were commonplace in the 1950s, 1960s, and 1970s, but both industries had become estranged from their filmmaking colleagues on the mainland.

Filmmaking in the People's Republic was nationalized in 1953 and soon developed into a highly centralized, rigidly controlled industry with provincial and urban studios all answering to the Central Film Bureau. Due to this consolidated control over both form and content, film expression was limited to the approved model of "socialist realism," which was a politically prescriptive rather than socially descriptive type of realism.

During the Cultural Revolution, film education and production came to a standstill. The mainland's only film school, the Beijing Film Academy, closed and the industry turned out only thirteen feature films between 1967 and 1974. By the late 1970s, the industry was beginning to recover and, with the return of higher education, the Beijing Film Academy reopened and accepted a new class (which included such international stars-to-be as Chen Kaige and Zhang Yimou).

In the same period, Taiwan's film industry experienced a downturn after having reached a high point producing genre films for domestic and Southeast Asian markets in the late 1960s and early 1970s. Despite continued striving by a few private production companies, the industry was centralized, with the state-owned, vertically integrated Central Motion Picture Corporation (CMPC) producing the majority of films. "Healthy realism," which aimed to shine a positive light on social reality through melodramas about the value of hard work and moral rectitude, was the dominant sensibility of the CMPC's productions.

Meant to motivate the populace, "healthy realism" promoted economic advancement, agricultural development, and regional self-government. This was about to change, however, slowly but irrevocably. Founded in the fifties, the Kuomintang-financed CMPC started to move away from serving merely as a mouthpiece for the government and into the production of movies that were more appealing to the masses and that more accurately reflected the nascent identity of Taiwan. Li Xing's *Beautiful Duckling* (1965) is an example of such landmark Taiwanese films.

One of the more influential figures on the Taiwanese film scene was not a filmmaker at all but a novelist, and a romance novelist·at that. Chiung Yao, whose bestsellers were made into more than fifty Taiwanese films, was perhaps the single most important constituent in forming the character of her nation's cinema, beginning with *Four Loves* in 1965 and extending through *The Light from Last Night* in 1983. In her dreamily romantic way, Chiung was a radical: her emphasis on love as life's raison d'être clashed with the more fundamentalist Taiwanese accent on family ethics and tradition. Her portrayal of marriage and family as the major obstacles to lovers' consummating their relationships helped westernize Taiwan and must have made Chiung all but revolutionary, as well as a favorite among the young.

Taiwan movies were still escapist entertainment (as was most of what came out of the contemporaneous Hollywood studio system), but a sea change in the island's cinema grew out of the work of the filmmaker Li Han-hsiang (formerly of Shaw Brothers). Li established the Grand Motion Picture Company and began to adapt Taiwanese literary works for the screen.

Taiwan was under Japanese domination from the late nineteenth century through the mid-twentieth century, and it was this period that saw the evolution of what Taiwan's literary historians call its native regional literature. This genre provided a basis for the development of the Taiwanese New Wave. *The Sandwich Man*, for instance, a portmanteau film from 1983 (its three directors included Hou Hsiao-hsien), was an adaptation of three short stories by the novelist Huang Chun-ming, a preeminent writer of Taiwanese nativist fiction and a leading translator of Chinese literature. Such literature encouraged directors to show the face of Taiwan, warts and all, as did the work of the so-called modernists, a group of novelists who, unlike the nativists, adopted Western literary innovations and westernized concepts such as individualism, rationalism, and liberalism. These modernists would later become screenwriters.

One such writer is Wu Nianzhen, who stars in Yang's *Yi Yi* but also wrote or cowrote many pivotal films. Wu wrote and directed *A Borrowed*

Life, which dealt with the virtual hero-worship of the Japanese by those growing up in prewar Taiwan. Contrast this with a film such as Wang Tong's *The Strawman,* which was about the intimate relationships between the rulers during the 1940s, when the Japanese were leaving and the Nationalists were coming, or with Hou's *A City of Sadness,* which also concerns the so-called February 28 incident and Taiwan's struggle against its new rulers. What you see in these films is a continuum of artistic expression against ongoing repression.

Edward Yang is a part of this, too, in his own particular way, although the repression he sees is often a self-made affliction, born of either avarice or apathy. It is true that he has made only two films that could be called period pieces (*A Brighter Summer Day* and the short *Expectations*). It is also true that *A Brighter Summer Day* was in many ways a profile of tangible cultural oppression. But Yang is, for the most part, a psychological portraitist whose westernized worldview makes him unique in Taiwan culture.

The social history of Taiwan is grounded in anxiety. The island's most influential population after 1949 was made up of more or less forced political refugees; one might imagine them, in the annals of colonization, somewhere between American-Dreamy fortune seekers and those who arrived in chains. The native population was forcibly mixed with a massive influx of mainland Chinese who would continue for years to consider their new home a temporary haven while still awaiting breathlessly the overthrow of Mao Zedong (and who were understandably resented by the native Taiwanese, while being cruelly misled by the Americans). The immigrants' children would grow up having their homeland derided by their parents as a wasteland, cultural or otherwise. And those children might have resented their parents, too.

What the place seemed to lack was unity, not so much of ethnicity but of political and cultural purpose. Chiang Kai-shek's hold on the Nationalist crowd was born as much of fear as devotion, and the cult of his personality was something that could not be shared by a younger generation, who could so easily recognize the desiccated corpse of Chiang's "charisma." The hypocrisy of the Chiang regime became the hypocrisy of the parents. The lack of something to fill the resulting void, the unfilled need for some kind of belief system, was the burden the children carried.

Strength through diversity carries a country only so far, even if it actually embraces the concept. As we have seen during the United States' campaign following the attacks of September 11, 2001, a slogan such as "United We Stand," while not entirely empty, is still all about who you are united against; it's about who you are not, as much as who you are. When people are disenfranchised, attacked, or made to feel impotent, socially or politically—as we also witnessed after September 11—they find something to validate their identity and to empower them, often with calamitous results.

Although not intended to promote "ethnic unity" or to amplify some other xenophobic anthem of a world unhinged, the ideas at the center of a film like Yang's *A Brighter Summer Day* are about this need for belonging, not just to a family but to a nation and, at last resort, to a gang. While the film implies a certain futility in the very quest it portrays, it also presumes a need among us for something more than tribal in the way our lives are connected to those of others. This presumes an awareness of the world at large and a recognition that the people of that world are peers.

Therefore, an Edward Yang film—unlike the films of, say, his onetime friend, collaborator, and fellow founder of the Taiwanese New Wave, Hou Hsiao-hsien—has to be viewed from a kind of partisan perspective, of the type held by an active participant in the process of life as lived the way most people live it (at least in the first and second worlds). It also requires a certain conviction that it is still worth subscribing to the ideals of those worlds (that is, tolerance, open-mindedness, and equality of the sexes/races/religions), however poorly realized they may be. Since the yearning for connections in a modern society, especially a modern society that seems predetermined to thwart that yearning, is an essential component of Yang's dramas, one cannot be uninvolved—or, perhaps more accurately, uninformed or poorly educated—and watch his films with the kind of awareness they demand.

Hardly anything is ever written about Yang without a mention of Hou Hsiao-hsien, which is understandable as they are among a handful of the world's great living directors and come from the same small island. But while they share some stylistic similarities—including use of the detached, static camera and a propensity for long shots and nonlinear narratives—Hou focuses on rural settings and male-centered stories almost exclusively, doesn't speak English, and hardly ever leaves Taiwan. The cosmopolitan Yang is a filmmaker of the city, of women, of cultural cross-pollination, who studied and worked in the United States for a number of years and views his homeland from the world at large.

The viola in the string quartet of famous Taiwanese filmmakers (Yang and Hou are the violins; Stan Lai is the cello) is Tsai Ming-liang. Tsai has certain things in common with his colleagues, aside from being born outside Taiwan (Tsai emigrated from Malaysia; Lai was born in Washington, D.C.). One is a talent for using the static camera to find humor and meaning. As has been said about its use by Hou, eventually something will happen. In Tsai's case, the result is often something very funny. Another commonality in their films is the inseparability of man and country. The nature of Taiwan, with its lack of homogeneous identity (like the United States), large immigrant population (like the United States), and subsequent cultural rootlessness (like the United States), is always part of Tsai's subject matter, the isolation of his characters, or his cult of the individual.

Tsai's filmmaking primarily grows out of a unique take on the endemic absurdity of the modern world, no more so than when the clean, lean narrative structures of his films are exploded by the patently outrageous (such as the songs of the Taiwan pop star Grace Chang as they punctuate *The Hole*). Tsai exists in an even more solitary realm than Yang and Hou. With a film by Hou, it is conceivable that the most insulated human could draw from his existential point of view an emotional payload mined from the pure cinematic asceticism the director often attains. But it is impossible to believe that a humanoid creature could emerge from a cave and grasp emotionally the conflicts at place in something like *A Brighter Summer Day*.

Hou has been described as the most Chinese of filmmakers—although Yang has blamed the pair's shared distribution problem on the possibility that they are "not Chinese enough." Hou operates contextually within the relatively limited perimeter of Taiwanese existence, which is not to disparage Hou in any way. He is in fact far more the critic's darling, the purity of his filmmaking—with its insistently uncompromised rhythms, long, meditative takes, and mournfully dour outlook—achieving for him a singular status among world cineastes. Yang is certainly a more "mainstream" director, more of a storyteller. But the bigger difference between Taiwan's two most prominent directors is in their worldviews. Yang's includes more of the world.

"Narrative" has become a loaded term; "corporate narrative," in fact, is a commodity. Take this pitch, offered on the Web site of an unnamed management consultant firm: "The 'corporate narrative' of any organization provides significant insight into its future effectiveness. Listening and learning from individual and communal stories provides the much needed context a leader can use to move an organization closer to its vision. Find out when and how to use such stories to communicate vision, values and meaning in narrative leadership: using the power of stories."

Critics of globalization, of unyielding advertising campaigns (or the single advertising campaign that makes up the résumé of untethered corporate power), find in the relentless selling of product the creation of narrative. A company selling corn flakes uses its purchased airtime not only to promote the idea that happy consumers devour their cereal but to create the associative connections between happiness and corn flakes. Companies such as General Electric (polluter of the Hudson River, manufacturer of nuclear arms and reactors) "bring good things to life" and tell us about it through sentimental but deftly structured advertisements that promote their beneficence. Their sins, of course, go unmentioned.

Governments do the same thing, naturally, creating a narrative of tribal unity and self-defense to justify unjustified wars, oil drilling, pipeline contracts, the selling out of national interests, and the stealing of elections. The narrative under which Yang and his generation grew up was about forced dislocation, the eventual retaking of the mainland, the patriarchal benevolence of Chiang Kai-shek, and faux unity.

Yang's mission has been the reclaiming, or recreation, of a national narrative.

What differentiates the two preeminent films in his oeuvre—*A Brighter Summer Day* and *Yi Yi*—from his other movies is the kind of one-worldism he assumes in the "lesser" films, as regards the problems of the human species. It isn't that the "modernism" of *Taipei Story* and *The Terrorizer* doesn't get to the heart of contemporary life and art and their inherent dilemmas; quite the contrary. But unlike *Brighter Summer Day* and *Yi Yi,* which encompass worlds so large in narrative scope and character that they can simply explain themselves, the others demand a certain acquaintance with how life is lived right now—the specifics, in other words. When the lovers Lon and Chin find themselves at romantic loggerheads in *Taipei Story*, which is as emotionally anxious a film as Yang has made, their situation is a reflection of very specific time, place, and moral atmosphere. Lon is caught on a generational fence, torn between what his girlfriend wants and deserves and the kind of man he has been raised to be: the conventional caveman/laissez-faire lover. And he knows it; indeed, these films are remarkable for the amount of self-awareness their characters possess.

The Lon-Chin conflict leads us unavoidably to the problematic attitude toward women contained in Yang's movies, an issue that is less about gender than it is about generations. It has often been noted that fathers are conspicuously absent in Yang films. They are absent spiritually, as are the callously manipulative fathers of *That Day, on the Beach*, or physically, as is Ming's missing father in *A Brighter Summer Day*, or both, as is the fugitive mobster dad in *Mahjong*. This reflects the vacuum of leadership that Yang sees in his country, as well as in its homes. But it's not as if mothers get any quarter from Yang.

Ming, the boy-hopping teenage siren of *A Brighter Summer Day*, has a mother who is not just an invalid but a weakling; she shamelessly avails herself of others' goodwill, compounding Ming's sense of humiliation and outrage. In the same film, S'ir's mother is not only too cheap to buy him eyeglasses, she's too self-absorbed not to express, out loud, the hope that she won't have to. In *Taipei Story*, Chin's mother is a mere shadow, downtrodden but—the implication is—also too cowardly to have protected her daughter from an abusive father. There is brutally judgmental motherhood in *That Day*, self-indulgent motherhood in *Yi Yi*, and hysterical motherhood in *The Terrorizer*.

And yet Yang (whose expressions of affection for his own mother are quite sincere) creates younger female characters of such profound complexity, nuance, and sympathy that we can only view the older women characters as devices for further examining the troubled heritage of Taiwan as a legacy of instability; the hand that rocks the Taiwanese cradle can barely be bothered to do so, it seems, preoccupied as a woman is with keeping her sanity.

The younger women of Yang's films are wildly complicated. Writing about *That Day, on the Beach*, the feminist Taiwanese writer Li Ang said, "It is a film which no woman who has grown up on the fringes of traditionalism and modernism should miss. Rather than call it a movie, I would be more willing to call it a 'document' of a Chinese woman, how she grows to be an independent and self-willed 'human being,' through her own efforts during a period of dramatic transformation in moral and social values. Of even greater relevance is the fact that it draws upon what we all know from everyday life; what it portrays is a woman's 'Chinese experience'" (Ou, chap. 4, 11–12).

Ching-ching, the pianist we meet in *That Day,* became a world-class artist because of a broken heart. What does this transition signify about art and love? Apparently, that a pedestrian romance can give birth to great music. Her friend, Jia-ji, whose privileged upbringing and tragic marriage lead to a self-realization of biblical proportions, is another source of complications. Ming, in *A Brighter Summer Day,* perhaps the most complex of Yang's creations, spends a childhood without a real home or financial security and under the constant threat of her mother's illness. Seemingly too young for such ruthlessness, but ruthless just the same, she finds security in guileless men who may seem dangerous but have nothing in their repertoire of cynicism and craft that can possibly compare with Ming's.

Yang's young women are a purer reflection than are his young men of what's afoot in the world, in particular, the world of multinational corporations, speculations, and alleged gender equality. Unequipped for the machismo that characterizes the social side of big business (and certainly not just in Asia), a woman like Chin, who hitches herself to a successful climber like Mrs. Wei in *Taipei Story,* still has to make choices between love and career, while burdened with very particular handicaps. As a woman, a careerist like Mrs. Wei is more or less excused from the requirements of mentorship that a male counterpart would be socially committed to fulfill. She makes it clear that she feels no responsibility to reward Chin's loyalty. She is a woman clawing her own way through a man's world, after all, and has the right—no, the obligation—to think only of herself.

But again, Mrs. Wei is the older woman, a minor character, and a lost cause. Yang uses her to illustrate Chin's plight, not to rail against the kind of world that produced a Mrs. Wei. But this is because Yang is a filmmaker who constantly looks forward in time. Whether this worldview marks him as an optimist, exactly, is debatable; in both *Taipei Story* and *That Day, on the Beach* the acknowledgement that the sins of the fathers were being visited upon the sons or daughters did not mean the sons or daughters were going to be any better off (far from it). But it certainly separates him from directors whose work attempts to reinvent the medium by reinterpreting the past. All past is prologue to Yang, which makes him an artist of eternal youth—or, at least, *for* eternal youth.

It also makes him essentially irreverent and an easy target of critics for whom a validation of the present requires a glorification of the past. In *A Brighter Summer Day*, but also in his other work, his stance is this: if the present isn't acceptable, then the past is responsible. In *Yi Yi* we have one character, NJ, trying to recapture his history while his daughter Ting-ting winds up reliving it. But the interesting thing about *Yi Yi* within the context of all Yang's work isn't just the constant presence and positive influence of the movie's father figure; it is the lack of causality between NJ's past and his daughter's. Fate, which in this film is less the result of outside factors and more the product of individual judgment and desire, just seems a kind of vortex in which one must swim or swirl.

It is not that way in *A Brighter Summer Day*, where a direct line of consequence connects the 1949 flight of the Nationalists from the mainland and the culminating murder, in 1960, of a teenage girl. Although *A Brighter Summer Day* signified a maturation of Yang's storytelling technique and a homing in on the points he really wanted to make about life in Taiwan generally and Taipei specifically, Yang is looking, via that film, for reasons for things that may be inexplicable. *Yi Yi* is a nod to the possibility that destiny may be utterly random.

This leads, unalterably, to the small-"n" nationalist's dead end. If fate is beyond our control, it is also beyond our ethnicity, race, religion, and country of origin. Random destiny unites us all. That is the ultimate irony, as embodied in the work of Edward Yang.

Expectations

Yang's first work made for theatrical release, *Expectations* (its title is sometimes translated as *Desires*), was one of the four shorts by four directors—the others being Tao Te-chen, Ko I-cheng, and Chang Yi—included in the anthology entitled *In Our Time* (*Guangyin de Gushi*), produced by the Central Motion Picture Corporation. It was a remarkable thing for the CMPC to have sponsored, considering the studio's reputation for rigid conservatism *and* the fact that the movie unleashed a new wave of filmmaking on Taiwan. But the local film industry was depressed, production-related ripoffs were common, and there seemed little reason not to give some younger directors a break.

Though unrelated thematically, the short films that comprise *In Our Time* represent separate stages of life and distinct historical periods, from primary school through early adulthood and from the agrarian 1960s through the modernized 1980s. *In Our Time* deals with social and economic issues in a way never before seen in Taiwanese films. The style of the four separate films would be described as realism, not the euphemistic "healthy realism" but life as actually lived by everyday people Taiwan. The films concerned themselves—as so much Taiwanese New Wave work would—with childhood and memory. Unlike the entrenched cinema, which strenuously avoided politics or social reality, *In Our Time* jumped in with both feet. Taiwan audiences responded as favorably as any audience might, upon seeing itself on screen for the first time.

Hsiao-fen, the subject of *Expectations* (*Zhiwang*, 1982), is a sort of prototype for the young Yang heroine. This is true of her appearance—the short-cropped hair, the crisp white blouses, the school-length skirts—as well as her bemusement at the vagaries of life. Physically, she foreshadows Ming in *A Brighter Summer Day* and, temperamentally and physically, she anticipates Ting-Ting in *Yi Yi*. She is the first thing we see, in closeup, when *Expectations* begins: sober but otherwise inscrutable. Is she sad, resigned, melancholic, an adolescent female in a repressed environment, or all of these?

All of these, of course. The younger of the two daughters of an overworked single mother, Hsiao-fen is entering womanhood without a visa and as if emerging from the dark, or, perhaps, into the dark. The movie's best known and probably pivotal scene takes place in the middle of the night, as Hsiao-fen is awakened by the onset of her first period. She looks under the sheets in confusion. Then she looks to her sister's bed. No one is there. She cries for her mother. No one comes. Whether

Shi Anni in
Expectations.

she knows what's going on or not is not entirely clear. What she does know is that she's alone.

What we know is arrived at almost entirely by deduction; Yang tells us almost nothing outright, working instead within known borders and with a generous palette of visual cues. Both the frankness and the almost fiercely economical way in which he tells a very simple story (with not-so-simple echoes) reconcile the title of the four pieces with the "in our times" of Hemingway and Turgenev. All share a modernist form of expression, stripped of unessential adornment and dwelling on matters vulgar, mundane, and illuminating. Both the subject and style set Yang's film apart from everything that had come before it in Taiwan film.

There is certainly a freewheeling, iconoclastic attitude in what Yang has to say. Hsiao-fen's closest friend, the squinty, bespectacled neighbor kid with whom we see her—he's much smaller, could be much younger, seems to be her only pal—is certainly no state-approved paragon of Taiwanese youth. Dressed in the standard-issue military-school uniform, he is obsessively concerned with basketball (and hopes someday to grow tall enough to play) while harboring mixed feelings about his education. ("I hate these recitations," he says.) The two obviously spend much time together; possibly, there is simply no one else around.

"Wouldn't it be nice if I could ride a bike," he says, listing the many things he could do if he would in fact learn to ride a bike.

Wang Qiguang (left)
and Shi Anni (right) in
Expectations.

"Go ahead and learn," she almost barks at him, adding, "don't make any of your usual excuses." They'll practice, she says, on Sunday.

Hasiao-fen is tough in her way, as so many of Yang's young women will be. But she also shares with them a solitude that is close to devastating.

Cut to the house: With the kind of stationary, deep-focus shot that would become a trademark, Yang gives us Hsiao-fen's mother in the family kitchen, her westernized 1960s bouffant adding five inches to her height. The Beatles are on TV; Sis, the older daughter, watches them sing "Ticket to Ride." Her mother upbraids her. "Find a job if you can't get into college next year," Mom tells Sis, suggesting her meal ticket will be canceled, as they reenact a universal scenario, the dinner table as theater of war.

There is a war on the TV, too, the Vietnam War. A B-52 drops a payload, a mini-mushroom cloud erupts, a Vietnamese man carries off a dead child in his arms. Hsiao-fen, looking over Sis's shoulder, grimaces at the carnage.

The girls' father has died, although it is not clear when, but "ever since, I've been working day and night," Mom says. Small battles, short tempers.

The pop music, the Vietnam coverage, the plight of the single mother, the portrait of what is considerably less than domestic bliss, intermural family strife, a storyline not based on romance—all this brought an almost documentary content to the Taiwanese feature, which is counterbalanced in *Expectations* by Yang's decidedly poetic rhythms.

The family discussion turns to the family's empty room. Their lodger has left; the room must be rented. Why don't you get a student, Sis asks. The girls you rent to always leave when they get married, she says. But why a student would not leave eventually, too, is unclear, except that Sis is thinking of students as males and males are something she's got on the brain.

Hsiao-fen watches as her sister dresses to go out—red dress, big earrings. The inference one takes is that Sis is on the prowl; when she comes home, she strips off her dress and crashes into bed. When Hsiao-fen rises, oh-so-drowsily, in the morning, she goes to the mirror, drops the top of her gown, and checks on the progress of her budding breasts. She looks less than encouraged.

Obviously, Hsiao-fen is in that amorphous state between girlhood and womanhood. Pushing her forward, a bit prematurely perhaps, is the arrival of the family's new lodger, a lanky, strikingly handsome male student, who sets the entire house atilt.

But first, a bike ride. Hsiao-fen and her little buddy spend the next Sunday in a field, trying to master the skills of the two-wheeler. Hsiao-fen holds the back of the bike as her friend gets his balance; when he does the same for her, however, she waves him off with irritation. She, in fact, masters the bicycle first.

Back home we hear the Beatles' "Hello Goodbye" (marking a farewell to at least one stage of her development). Hsiao-fen tells Sis about the lodger. "Really?" she remarks. "What does he look like?" At breakfast, he comes to the door to pay the rent. Hsiao-fen is transfixed.

Her attitude, communicated almost entirely though the actress Shi Anni's facial expressions, changes toward her little friend. The lodger has a motorcycle (mobility being a major metaphor in *Expectations*); her pal can't even ride a bike. The little guy embarrasses her, suddenly; between her sister and her friend, Hsiao-fen feels imprisoned in a sexual limbo.

Although we are not fully aware of it, Yang is condensing the entirety of adolescence into a short few days. "I don't feel well," Hsiao-fen says one night. "Go to bed early, then," her sister says (her words foreshadowing those of the mother in *A Brighter Summer Day,* who prescribes early bedtime for bad eyesight). Once her period comes, Hsiao-fen is officially a woman—officially, if not emotionally. She does her homework but drifts into a reverie about the lodger. One afternoon, while the women of the house are working outside, the lodger arrives home, shirtless, glistening with perspiration, a basketball under his arm. Hsiao-fen is now officially stunned. Mom asks him to move some cinderblocks. As he carries them, we get Hsiao-fen's near-comical point of view: His rangy self. Then her face. Then his torso. Then her face. Then his torso, now in slow motion. Her face. His torso. His torso. His torso—finally, her face. We see her sister's face, too, wearing a comparable look of mesmerization.

"When did you start liking boys?" Hsiao-fen asks Sis, who cuts her down with a contemptuous glance of boredom. Hsiao-fen is embarrassed. The little guy, meanwhile, is still at it. He comes by the next day to borrow the bike, rides it, and crashes again.

Hsiao-fen, at her homework, mentally rehearses asking the lodger for help with her studies. But as she actually approaches the rented room, she hears voices. Carefully sliding a window open, she sees the lodger in bed, bare-chested again, and her sister clad in only a shirt. What she sees then, we do not. But we do get Hsiao-fen's mortified look, as she retreats from the window.

It is a retreat that continues, Yang suggests. Hsiao-fen has had her life lesson, and the next time we see her, she is back in the alley where the film began, at night—maybe the same night—as she is approached by the little guy on the bike. She all but ignores him, but he is unfazed. Look, he says, riding down the alley but crashing again.

The cliché would be for Hsiao-fen to be cruel, but she is not. It is as if, having seen what her sister did, she would rather hold on to her childhood a little bit longer. We leave with the little guy talking about what he will do when he finally grows—play basketball, ride to school. He can't wait to grow up. At this point, however, she can.

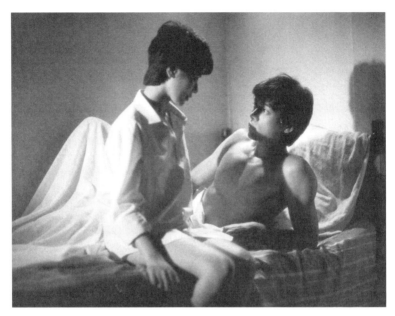

Zhang Yingzhen (left) and Sun Yadong (right) in
Expectations.

That Day, on the Beach

The beach in Yang's first feature represents what Rosebud did in Orson
Welles's: that ineluctable and elusive moment when life was perfect—
and a symbol of everything that went wrong.

There are many points on which we can compare *That Day, on the
Beach (Haitan De Yitian,* 1983) to *Citizen Kane* (although Yang's debut
feature is the one in his filmography that most resembles Antonioni's
works, a comparison he apparently hates). But the most important similarity is this: the film presents a filmmaker fully formed, one as adept
with the stylistic facets of storytelling as he is with storytelling itself.

A tour de force of time and memory, *That Day,* much like *Kane,*
begins as a mystery. At the close of day, backlit by a bleeding sun, a
silhouetted figure runs across the shoreline, taking something he has
found to show to another. The second man's uniform cap is also framed
by the light. The officer inspects the object with great attention. What

is it? It takes nearly three hours before we are really sure, and the closing of the gap between our knowledge and that of the characters is the heart of the film's experience.

Yang establishes several personal tropes in *That Day, on the Beach* (the carefully punctuated title of which, in English at least, presents the film with an oddly appropriate delicacy). They are devices that will mark much of his later work. One such device is the use of a minor or even marginalized character—in *That Day* it is Jia-sen, a disappointed doctor and the brother of the lead character, Jia-ji—as the fulcrum of the story. (Siblings seem to give Yang what he needs to ornament his work; Ling, the sister of Chin in *Taipei Story,* is another good example.) Another characteristic is Yang's focus on the predominant role Western culture plays in Taiwan, something that will strongly mark his initial masterpiece, *A Brighter Summer Day.* At the same time, *That Day* is a critique of old-style Taiwanese culture, which is shown to be content to sacrifice the happiness of children on the altar of their parents' propriety. (One father, having gotten both his children engaged to perfectly unsuitable people, sighs, "That's a weight off my mind.") But at the same time, Yang never launches such a critique with a presumption that free will necessarily makes for happier endings.

The entire opening of *That Day* is a red herring. A pianist named Ching-ching prepares for an evening concert. Checking the action on her newly tuned piano, she requests some readjustments, expressing the hope that they'll be made by showtime. You suspect they will.

Ching-ching is a clearly disaffected, and much celebrated, character. After being harried by her assistant to make it to rehearsal, a press conference, and a post-concert cocktail party, that same assistant gives her a note that stirs her from her self-absorption.

There is a flashback (the first of dozens) to a rugby scrum. A young woman is framed by the swarm of departing players, who pay her little notice as she passes among them. Back to the pianist; Ching-ching is musing. We have entered her personal honeycomb of memory.

But while it may be a personal reminiscence, it isn't exclusively hers. One of the hallmarks of *That Day, at the Beach*—indeed, of the entire Yang oeuvre—is that the director moves gracefully and effortlessly between characters and time frames (such ease connoting, of course, the greatest amount of effort). Gliding from one flashback to another, yet always rooting us in the present, he makes contemporary time indissoluble from the past and one memory indissoluble from another.

Like a pianist himself, Yang varies his attacks, revealing the various worlds within the upper-middle-class Taipei universe that is the stage for *That Day.* There is Jia-sen, a young medical student who is having trouble in dissection class, an implication that he's doing something he finds repulsive. But his father is a doctor. His father's best friend is a doctor. And he's not only going to be a doctor himself, he's going to marry his father's best friend's daughter. Jia-sen's life is choreographed, move by move (much as Yang's probably was, when he toed the Taiwanese line and went off to engineering school), and so is that of his sister Jia-ji, although she will take a different path. Jia-sen, sought out by Jia-ji following the parental deal-cutting, is seen repeatedly hurling a ball against a wall and catching it in his mitt, thoroughly absorbed in his anger. While the mountains behind him suggest a classical Asian miniature, a painterly synthesis of old world and new, Jia-sen solo is an equally perfect portrait of future misery.

Ching-ching reappears, solemn as always, her assistant audible in voice-over saying, "I'll take care of the press conference . . ." The window of her limousine bisects her face, exposing part of it while the foliage rushing by is reflected in the bottom half of the glass. Dualities—as we will see later, and most emphatically, in *Yi Yi*—are multitudinous in Yang's work, and Ching-ching's personal dichotomy is the first to be examined.

"I tried more than once to get in touch with you," the older Jia-ji tells Ching-ching across a table at a Taipei cafe. Why has this meeting been sought? As it turns out, it is only because of the men who are in—or now out of—their lives. Ching-ching had loved Jia-sen but was deemed unsuitable by his family. It was that very rejection that sent her into a concert career.

"All I wanted to do was make a little money teaching and to wait for Jia-sen to graduate," she says. After his engagement to another woman, however, "All that was left was the music."

There are any number of things going on here. Ching-ching has become world famous (we assume) as a direct result of her rejection as a suitable match for marriage. Her artistry, presumably, was also born of that trauma. Is Yang suggesting that a strangling control exerted

Terry Hu (left) and Sylvia Chang in *That Day, on the Beach.*

over children by their parents is the mother of art and success? Would Ching-ching still rather be married to Jia-sen than famous? (She would, as it turns out.) Or is the fate of Jia-ji—who will not marry her parents' choice and will live to regret it—testament to the wisdom of old-line Taiwanese matchmaking?

Frankly, we are not entirely sure.

It is not the kind of dilemma in which the older Yang will find himself; as his filmmaking develops, his ability to resolve conflicting ideas—or to avoid situations where ideas would conflict—becomes far more nimble.

At the same time, Yang is developing themes, for instance, using the music of Elvis Presley, who is heard singing "Hound Dog" while Jia-ji's persona is being established, as she's seen in school, with friends, or with boys. A misinterpreted Presley lyric will supply the title for *A Brighter Summer Day.*

While inside the home, which should be a sanctuary, fates are manipulated, outside, in the rain, striations on the wall of a building are illuminated in a diffused halo of light. The image is a reflection of the social world of Taiwan, the rigidly conformist nature of its society framed by a symbol of an unpredictable universe. (Yang, the ultimate woman's director, might also be calling up Claude Chabrol's use of parallel lines in *Les Bonnes Femmes*.)

Jia-ji has met De-wei, the fiancé chosen by her parents; they go to the marriage bureau and are wed among a crowd of fellow applicants. We don't get the wedding; we don't even quite see the young lovers hold hands. Yang is off again, back to the cafe where Ching-ching and Jia-ji seem to be sharing each other's memories. *That Day* as the title implies, has never ceased to echo.

In a way, we have been set up for a two-way examination of fractured romance. The film begins with Ching-ching, a far more logical subject for drama; she's famous, temperamental, an artist. Instead, Yang focuses on Jia-ji, who for most of the movie, and for most of her life, is a far more pedestrian character. But the obvious—and the glamorous, and the instantly intriguing—is of little interest to Yang. A deeper experience is.

"Something happened three years ago," Jia-ji says. "De-wei drowned." We flash to Jia-ji screaming her way to the beach.

Yang shifts into a kind of talking-heads mode: fishermen deliver their accounts of a strange man on the beach, who waded into a sea that was too cold for swimming but just right for drowning. A pill vial—a prescription for some psychiatric medication—is found, bearing De-wei's name. Jia-ji knew nothing about any medications, or psychiatrists. But she knew De-wei was troubled.

So we flash back again—or is it forward?—to the early days of the marriage of Jia-ji and De-wei (Ching-ching has, at this point, effectively left the picture). They both work at a newspaper, she as a translator; we see her being abused by her boss. When the two leave the paper we see them running along the beach. It's the Rosebud scene, the moment when everything was as perfect as it was going to get and, of course, no one involved ever knew it.

Blame it on biography, if you will. Taiwan is arguably a land whose entire subtext is a stratum of regret (for land lost, potential squandered, culture abandoned). Yang's films may possess a Proustian respect for memory, but it is mixed with a Faulknerian sense that we can never escape history's grasp.

De-wei, predictably enough, gets a better job and the couple's life together starts to unravel. As per Asian business culture, after-work drinking, to the point of regurgitation, is not just encouraged but required. Pampered and useless, Jia-ji takes flower-arranging courses. On the couple's third anniversary, the maid leaves the phone off the hook and De-wei, drafted into celebrating his firm's new account, can't reach Jia-ji to say he won't be home for dinner. It is a meal that Jia-ji has cooked and that provides the compost upon which the dissolution of their marriage can root and blossom.

Yang does some heavy-handed moralizing, and *That Day, at the Beach* owes much to daytime drama. Structurally, however, it is brilliant. The director moves fluidly and movingly from past to present (the cafe) to a further past and then back again, creating a world of seamless time and simulacrity, a modality of the visible. You could watch it without dialogue (or subtitles), because the visual storytelling is solid.

Unwilling to accept De-wei's philandering, Jai-ji commits the ultimate sin, embarrassing him in front of his colleagues by following him to a job site, a wasteland of industrial agitation that lies like a scorched plain on the edge of Taipei. But De-wei's distress is actually a sign of his good nature, his humanity. Like Lon, the character Hou Hsiao-hsien plays in Yang's *Taipei Story,* he is a member of that postfeminism generation of men (like Yang himself) who have been thwarted by their own self-awareness. In the sexual arena, they know how they should act and what constitutes defensible behavior. But when society, or even a fragment of it, endorses self-indulgence, they find it very difficult to mount resistance.

For De-wei, whose sense of his manhood is linked to his after-hours drinking, his marriage is not just a damaged relationship but a representation of his damaged conscience; he begins to see Jia-ji, you suspect, as a walking recrimination. When he takes her on a death-defying drive through the traffic of downtown Taipei, frightening her (and us) half to death, there's no reason to think he's just trying to make a point. But he does stop at a red light; he can't push propriety quite that far. The answer to De-wei's enigmatic character becomes clear: he is constitutionally incapable of living his own life.

Jia-ji, doing the only thing she can, goes shopping. What follows is the scene at the beach, the first of those seemingly transcendent moments that punctuate each Yang film. In this case the ocean seems to pulsate as Jia-ji walks down that beach, virtually smothered under a sky of Antonioni blue. Some personal effects have been found, including the prescription bottle for the psychiatric medication that Jia-ji knew nothing about, issued in De-wei's name. A cop wants her to sign a form attesting to De-wei's suicide, but she's unsure whether to write him off quite so quickly. The cop is frustrated, a symbol of gross efficiency. "Only you could really know," he says, referring to her husband's state of mind. But then she realizes she doesn't know anything. She leans over for a light . . . and sits up back in the cafe, present tense attained. It is a marvelous juxtaposition. And she is a marvelous character. Jia-ji's epiphany, which soon will be assisted by her dying brother Jia-sen, is that there is no trust; nothing is not temporal; no one lives who doesn't live alone. But she becomes her own person in this crucible of insecurity and pain. Ching-ching can see it in her face.

Yang moves us back in time again; it is his least eloquent gesture, but it brings us to Jia-ji and Ping-ping, the younger man with whom she has a flirtation amid De-wei's dissolution, and her discovery of her husband's longtime affair with a calculating and ultimately coldhearted coworker. Jia-ji changes her hairstyle before her rendezvous with Ping-ping, but his lack of appreciation is all Yang needs to show us what Ping-ping is made of. She'll skip out on a subsequent meeting with Ping-ping knowing finally that he, like her father—who on his death bed can talk only of her brother—is unworthy of her. In this he is like De-wei, of whom she knows so little.

The movie is an epic, although of an uncertain nature. It certainly isn't historical, except in Taiwanese social terms. It isn't a romance, although there's romance in it. It is really just a saga of the self—Jia-ji's journey and education providing a roadmap from delusion to determination, over the landscape of her soul. As his own writer, and one who at this stage is probably more certain of himself on the page than on screen, Yang employs the most novelistic of devices, mistakenly (or not) misaddressed letters. There is one that De-wei wrote to his wife but sent to his mistress, another written to his mistress and mailed to his wife (the mistress later derides Jia-ji for her "storybook" upbringing). It is a great scene, but one whose impact relies on content rather than delivery.

The opposite is true of a subsequent scene in which Jia-ji's mother, visiting after her daughter's collapse at flower-arranging class, drinks her tea and then covers the cup. It's a deadly gesture, a poisonous dismissal of a daughter who has "failed." Yang then gives us the younger woman in her purest state, as a perplexed four-year-old listening to her father's Western music (much as Yang did as a boy), and then on a kind of hallucinatory tour of the equally baffling adult world, various aspects of which are contained in separate rooms. Peering in, she sees sexual encounters and betrayal but understands nothing, of course; it is Yang's way of saying that innocence offers no protection from the snares and wounds of the life to come.

After De-wei's disappearance, his old mistress accuses him of having embezzled company money and then fleeing to Japan, a story that gets to Jia-ji through De-wei's oldest friend and boss. De-wei is a sort of sacrifice to Jia-ji's education: he is in the sea, but Jia-ji, leaving the beach before the body is found, doesn't care anymore. She never knew him well enough to know what he might have done, and at this point, it

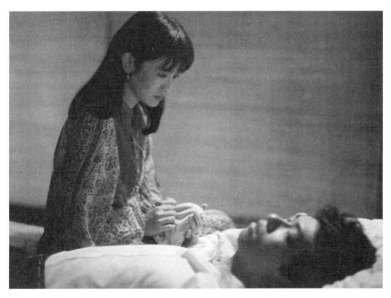

Sylvia Chang (left) and David Mao in *That Day, on the Beach.*

doesn't matter. "There could be any number of possible explanations," someone says. But to the new Jia-ji, none is of suitable consequence to alter her course.

In the end we are back to Jia-sen, who got a career he didn't want and lost the woman he did, and who goes out leaving Jia-ji with the summation of his life's story: "Everything depends on yourself." He dies in bed. The body of De-wei is recovered from the sea. Both men, it seems, laid down their lives for Jia-ji.

Taipei Story

Taipei Story (*Qingmei Zhuma*, 1985) was Yang's second full-length feature and won him a critic's prize at Locarno in 1985. More important, however, it displayed a markedly greater maturity than did *That Day, on the Beach* and revealed a greater certainty about what the director wanted to say. The film offered a broader statement about Taiwan and a realization of how one could tell multiple stories simultaneously.

Rather than depending on the numerous if graceful flashbacks/flash-forwards and the playfulness with time that he showed in *That Day*, Yang manipulates layers of meaning in *Taipei Story*. He creates a wide-ranging social critique while fashioning a character drama that might have worked as a film, even without such great psychological depth. In fact, a shallower movie might have done better commercially. Not surprisingly, *Taipei Story* was not very popular with Taiwan audiences, probably because of the cool detachment of its characters and tone. In it, Yang portrays people at their most alienated.

"The box office was pretty bad," Yang said in 2001. He continued:

> But also a lot of people didn't understand the intention of the film. They wanted to see another *Day on the Beach*, a love story with all these romantic entanglements. So they were put out when they looked at this movie. "What? You call this a love story? People breaking up?" But's that's how I looked at the city at the time—we were breaking away from the past and our ties to the past are inevitably romantic ones. But realities set in, economic pressures, other kinds of hardships. . . . But there weren't that many sophisticated critics at the time, and they tended just to discount the film as a commercial failure.

But looking back, what *Taipei Story* actually shows is my devotion to the place—how tied I feel to its past, but also how much I care about its future. ("Taiwan Stories" 133)

Taipei Story is, on one hand, a tale of star-crossed lovers. Lon and Chin—he, a former baseball player who ends up working in the family fabric store; she, an executive assistant to Mrs. Wei, the head of an architecture corporation—can't seem to find a way to make their romance work. In fact, they can't seem to get out of their own way, which turns out to be a major theme in much of Yang's work: the near impossibility of love, especially in a world in which happenstance and others' self-interest work so strenuously against it. It is something he also portrayed, for example, in *That Day, on the Beach*, probing the vagaries of the love/sex game in an arena where the rules are always changing.

Chin is a dissatisfied woman; in Yang's world, of course, to be a woman is to be dissatisfied. We meet Chin and Lon while they're apartment hunting—although they do it in such a half-hearted fashion as to deflate the hopes of the most optimistic real-estate agent.

The windowed doors that are shown in the opening shots of *Taipei Story,* and the size of the one room in the apartment in which they're framed against the light, foreshadow a similar room in *The Terrorizer.* Even the shape of the room is the same, as if to suggest that the limits on the options open to Taiwanese youth extend to the architecture itself. There are no shots fired, no police raid, no gambling den waiting to be shot into dust. Just a couple looking for an apartment, albeit without much enthusiasm.

She asks specifics about the rental; she wants shelves. He takes a few practice batting swings in the living room; he's going to America, the land of baseball and gunfire. Chin is sullen, clearly implying that the patriarchy she encounters at work and at home is so pervasive she couldn't be otherwise. She is shown repeatedly on the phone, as if to emphasize her disconnect from actual human contact. Yang's point throughout the film is that money, not love, is the engine of Taipei. It is true of any city, really, but of Taipei in particular. He shows it through the physicality of the place, in its glass and steel and empty reflections, as well as in the emotional distance between his characters.

Chin drives to work. At the office, she asks about the guys she sees in suits, anonymous junior-executive types who are clearly there for no good. Which is the boss? The guy in the glasses, she is told. They've all got glasses. They're corporate clones.

This brief segment is a funny aside, although Yang withholds the humor from his main characters, who are as dour in *Taipei Story* as anyone in any Yang film. This is his most somber movie, spearheaded by a tremendous performance by—once again—the future director Hou Hsiao-hsien as Lon, the washed-up, disillusioned baseball player who can't quite connect with the love of his life. Yang purposely chose nonprofessionals to star in the film; opposite Hou, the chanteuse Tsai Chin has the female lead.

"In *That Day, on the Beach*," Yang told the *New Left Review*,

> I wove together a lot of things that happened to me or my friends, making a kind of narrative structure out of our experience. The movie was very successful, but people often said that's because you have the support of all these stars in it. So in my second film, I wanted to break through my own limitations.
>
> One way of doing that was to have no stars, so I decided to use only

Ke Yizheng (left) and Tsai Chin in *Taipei Story*.

amateurs. Another was to create a story out of nothing—something that was not based on my own experience, or that of anyone else I knew. So my starting point was essentially conceptual. I wanted to tell a story about Taipei. There's a personal element to that: A lot of people have tried to brand me as a mainlander, a foreigner who's somehow against Taiwan. But I consider myself a Taipei guy—I'm not against Taiwan. I'm for Taipei. I wanted to include every element of the city, so I really gave myself a hard time, to build a story from the ground up. The two main characters represent the past and the future of Taipei and the story is about the transition from one to the other. I tried to bring enough controversial questions onto the screen, so the viewers would ask themselves about their own lives when they'd seen the film.

On the surface, *Taipei Story* offers a kind of poetic or even melodramatic façade. But actually, every element of the way we lived then was in the film. So that was the intention. (Interview 132)

It is a rather daring experiment Yang undertakes, the depiction of broad social change through the prism of intersecting conflicts and settings. Repeated shots of empty rooms symbolize the void in the characters' lives. Elsewhere, Yang is ironic; the film's Chinese title, translated as *Green Plum and Bamboo Stalk,* refers to an acclaimed T'ang poem by Li Bo, which celebrates the undying nature of young love, something about which the movie has a decidedly more jaded view.

The title of *Taipei Story* prompts what one supposes is an inevitable comparison with Ozu's *Tokyo Story,* a film with which Yang was no doubt familiar and to which he pays homage with shots made at Ozu level—about knee-high—or with shots that so obviously avoid that "subservient" perspective that you can't help thinking of Ozu anyway. But where the old master's film was about the abandonment of the elderly, either literally or figuratively, Yang's film is about the near-criminal neglect of the young by the people who have created their world; it is about that and the young people's own apathetic reaction to what is springing up around them and governing their lives.

Taipei Story is also, principally, about Taipei, a city of violent contrasts: Chin's apartment versus her parents' old home; Lon's antiquated fabric shop versus Chin's modern office; westernized bars versus Japanese karaoke; Lon's more traditional relationships versus the promiscuous ones of Chin's sister, Ling. The primary dichotomy at work, within the jungle that has become the city, is between those who can keep up, such as Chin, and those who can't. In the latter category is Chin's father and, ultimately, Lon.

The city's corporeal self affords a similarly dichotomous relationship to other major urban centers. Unlike the endearing, embracing construction of a Paris, or the lovable eccentricity of a crazy-quilt New York, Taipei and its architecture are seen as an element in its people's alienation. Chin's colleague Ko, who has half-hearted designs on her, bemoans the buildings that blight their city's skyline. "I can't even remember which ones I've designed," he says, taking the profile of his city as a personal affront. "It's as if it doesn't matter if I exist or not."

Yang is no naif; this kind of "why do I exist" whine is hardly new to movies or to the world. However, his point is not so much that an architect might question the value of his existence, but that the architecture surrounding him might prompt him to do it. It's a one-two punch. Urban man, Yang posits, exists in harmony, or not, with the city that surrounds him; in fact, he finds part of his identity through that city. (Even crossing the street can be a major existential problem for the Taiwanese. At one point, Chin tries to join Lon across a boulevard but the traffic, pulsing with a Mondrian-like, *Broadway Boogie Woogie* rhythm, keeps her at bay.) In the case of Taipei, the city-as-composition is a slap in the face to individuality.

But so are many cities. "What's L.A. like?" Lon is asked, and he answers, "Like Taipei: all these people from Taiwan. They sit and watch TV all day." Like De-wei in *That Day, on the Beach,* Lon is the perfectly muddled modern male, confused, in flux.

Back in Taipei after his trip to Los Angeles, Lon renews his "relationship" with Chin as well as with her father, another of those marginal Yang characters who nonetheless are essential to the message of the film in question. Chin's father is in trouble with gamblers. Games are a kind of poison. Lon is a man of action—of a sort. But baseball (the Yankee caps bob through the movie on various heads like dunce caps) is not just an American import, like so much of what constitutes Taiwanese culture in Yang's film. It is also a boy's game, one that preoccupies grown men to the point of infantilization. So do games of any kind—and to varying degrees of severity and sacrifice. Chin's father has taken his gamesmanship to an extreme, life-threatening degree, getting in debt to gamblers who won't take "tomorrow" for an answer and who come to Lon to get their money. Lon, in turn, sacrifices his and Chin's chance for a life in America in order to keep her dad from harm. Or is it just to make himself look good among the guys? She doesn't understand. No one does, including Lon.

Chin's father is an antiquated but hardly harmless influence on what circulates around him. From the tyrannical "Get me a beer" he barks at Chin to his summary of his business philosophy ("If you don't cheat, you can't make a profit"), he is a symbol of commercial oppression. In his failed business he made bottle caps and plastic tubing; maybe no one cares if he shortchanges his customers by undercutting standards. He isn't threatening anyone's life, after all. But that is a specious argument, one that ignores the need for personal responsibility or honor, qualities that seem to be missing from much of the day-to-day life of Yang's Taipei. And it is an argument that is treated, via the naked stare of his camera, with the contempt it deserves.

At the same time, it is a young man's contempt; the later Yang, the older Yang, will treat the same kind of flawed character as more symp-

Hou Hsiao-hsien (left) and Tsai Chin in
Taipei Story.

tomatic of the Taipei business world's systemic corruption. He will view the conditions that promote criminality as the rules of the game rather than the fault of the individual players.

After Chin has served the beer, the "boys" go out, leaving Chin at home. She finds her mother working inside the house. The woman is crouched in daunting shadows that nearly obscure her, making her almost indistinguishable from the house that has served so long as her prison. Chin makes a comment about Lon. "The price of vegetables is up again," her mother replies. If there is a joke there, it's pretty subtle and deftly delivered, but Yang seem more intent on illuminating the virtually unbridgeable gap between two generations, two worlds, than on making jokes that might get lost in the subtitles.

There is always a temptation to look for the cut and dried between the old and the new. Lon knows the delineations—as Hou makes us painfully aware through his performance. The question seems to be about the nature of weakness. What makes you weak, succumbing to a woman or to the traditions of men? Lon is himself aware of the friction between old and young, between the sexes, about what he owes Chin, about right and wrong.

Chin's mother gets no fleshing out from Yang, but then she serves mainly as a kind of mute relic, whose abuse at the hands of her husband casts her—and her subservient station in the household—as obsolete. (Chin, we hear later, was beaten while trying to protect her mother from her father, thus also showing the mother in a somewhat negative light for allowing her child to be abused on her behalf.) At the same time, Chin is not much better off. Her self-definition is linked to her job and to her role as executive assistant to the imperious Mrs. Wei.

But that new team of suits—remember those suits?—has stormed the barricades, waging corporate war with the napalm of downsizing. "Our management structure won't be the same as what you were used to," Chin is informed. What we need, she is told more bluntly, are secretaries. Proudly, Chin takes a walk.

Youth in limbo: Chin is in limbo as much as Lon is. Lon's man-boy status is similar in nature to Chin's undefined station as executive assistant and its meaninglessness in terms of power. And, of course, there's her status as a woman as well. The architect, Ko, asks her out again, for a beer. "Beer," she snaps. "Is that your excuse or your obsession?" She may be a new woman, but she would still like to meet a man who would cut to the chase. As in so many of Yang's films, the female is not just the nobler and/or more dangerous of the species. She is the beast of socio-sexual-cultural burden. Lon has lied to her; he didn't just transit through Tokyo on his way back to Taiwan; he stopped for a week, as he confides to one male friend (and not to Chin) to see his old girlfriend, Gwen. Chin goes out with the architect, who eats liver noodles. Going home to his wife and child, with whom he seems profoundly disenchanted, Ko dutifully eats a dutifully served plate of . . . liver noodles. His wife may not be consciously seeking revenge with dinner, but still it's a dish served hot.

Chin goes home to Lon, who is watching tapes of Dodger games he has brought back from the States, "I get home so late and you don't even ask where I've been," she says angrily. "What did you say?" he asks, absentmindedly. She probably wants to kill him, but at the same time Lon is in a bind, aware of the snare that any intelligent man of Yang's generation knows is waiting for him when dealing with intelligent women. Should he ask where she's been? Is it his business? Will he be committing patriarchal violations of her privacy if he questions what she's been up to?

In this case, not to ask shows an apathy that can only be insulting to Chin. Still, the question lingers: would Lon presume a kind of propri-etary air by "grilling" her? Chin is as confused as Lon is, though, and their mutual confusion serves as a kind of template for sexual relation-ships in the modern era.

Their disconnection from each other is reflected in their disconnec-tion from their increasingly materialistic society, and this same distancing is reflected in their physical appearance. Both are exotics, ethnically Chinese but not quite; the actress Tsai Chin, in the right light, could be black and/or Asian; Hou Hsiao-hsien has such strong facial features he might be Native American. Their nonspecific ethnicity, or pan-ethnicity, serves to set their characters apart even further from the ebb and flow of Taipei society, casting them as both alien and universal totems of a world in which love is impossible.

Yang gives us worlds—personal worlds—poised between hard-edged reality and escapist nonsense. The problem is there's no in-between, no gray areas, in the places where most people actually live. Life in Taipei is so black-and-white there is no room to breathe. When Lon accompanies Chin to a gathering with some colleagues from her company, Lon is humiliated at the dinner. "You're in textiles?" he is asked repeatedly, after explaining that his family's shop is an unfashionable fabric store in the town's old quarter. Lon's questioner is a smart-ass exec named Allen (the English name being something of a dig) and he presses Lon to play darts for money. "If not money, then time," Allen offers, taking Lon for something like four hundred hours until Lon just assaults him and a melee breaks out between Lon and Allen's fellow execs. The point is not so much that Lon reverts to violence to preserve his dignity. It is that Allen represents the substitution of money for what is traditionally perceived as manhood.

Using music, sports, and fashion, Yang constantly emphasizes the influence of America on Taipei. But Lon and Chin come the closest of any Yang characters to actually getting there (Lon goes but returns). With Chin's father having destroyed their chance to emigrate, the possibility is raised that Lon's brother-in-law might help them get over. But the brother-in-law was no help to Lon in business; in America, he would take Lon to a ballgame or out shooting—what else do they do there?

Again, Yang almost makes a joke: what could more stereotypically represent life in America than baseball and guns? But there's nothing lighthearted about how Lon depicts his stay or his host. His brother-in-law (whom we never see) went free after killing a black man. "In America," Lon says, grimly monotonal and deliberate, "if you see someone suspicious in your yard, you can shoot him dead, drag him inside, put a gun in his hand. That's called self-defense."

At this point, Mrs. Wei reappears, less than supportive of Chin than Chin would like and certainly not offering her a job in any new venture. "What about you and Ko?" she asks, admonishing Chin about any real or imagined office liaisons and presuming, because of their past affiliation, that although she has no obligation to give Chin work, she can still advise her about her private life. "And what about Lon?" Mrs. Wei asks, with arch hypocrisy. She may have gotten where she is by sidestepping conformity, not adhering to the feminine norm, and becoming something of the stereotypically brittle career gal. But she still promotes domestic bliss, even if very little domestic bliss is evident in Yang's Taipei.

Edward Yang has usually expressed concern for a younger generation, one more rootless than his own. Chin's sister, who comes to Chin for money for an abortion, is an example of the director's intentionally marginalized major characters. There is no excuse for making the sister part of the story he's telling, except that she is, in her way, essential to it. She represents another extreme, the hedonistic end result of a suffocating first generation and disaffected second. Completely footloose, she exists on the fringe of the story because she exists on the fringe of life. Her existence is virtually evanescent; she has no substance, partly because she chooses to have none.

In *Taipei Story,* there is also a cabbie, who rams Lon's car from behind. You expect the worst, but he is just an old pal who has fallen on hard times—emphasizing the growing gap between rich and poor as well as the self-destructive nature of a society with money in its heart. "Where's your wife?" Lon asks. "Still gambling?" The cabbie simply nods.

The cabbie is another fringe figure. Because he was tall as a kid, he was "groomed for Williamsport" (the annual site of the Little League World Series, in which Taiwan has traditionally been a contender). But he never grew any taller; his talent was stillborn, his arm ruined by throwing curve balls at a tender age. "I know when it's going to rain," he says. In a particularly pained scene, Lon offers gives him money and, after only modest resistance, he takes it.

Likewise, Chin gives taxi money to her mother, who instead takes the bus. There is a cherishing of cash for cash's sake, of security in money, not for what it can buy but for the safety it provides. It offers a comfort one finds nowhere else in life.

Lon and Chin seem meant for each other, but a force keeps pulling them apart. Mostly, that force can be described as the sins of the fathers—but also of the mothers and daughters. Lon at one point takes the cabbie's kids with him, in order to bring their mother home—by force as it turns out—from a gambling den. Chin's father, of course, is hiding from his debtors. And Gwen, Lon's old girlfriend, does her best to get between them.

"I always thought that she should be a boy," Gwen says of Chin, to which Lon replies curtly, "It shows how much you know about her." But his response actually shows how little *he* knows about her. After all, her aspirations and toughness and willingness to mix it up in business (or with her father) are, and always have been, unsuitable qualities for a Taipei woman. Perhaps she *should* have been a boy.

In the end, it is Gwen's relative femininity that blinds Lon to Chin's superior qualities. And when Chin slaps him for betraying her, his reaction is far out of proportion to what she has done. There's a tremor running throughout the picture that throws everything into disequilibrium. Lon's epiphany ends with him back in a bar gambling; Chin ends up with some bikers who know her sister, Ling. Their positions reverse: Chin parties and rides around town (and, quite pointedly, passes under a statue of Chaing Kai-shek). The newly responsible Lon takes care of the cabbie's family. At a disco (where "Footloose," one of the more irritating American pop records ever made, is playing), the lights go out. A kind of quiet humanity settles in. Then the lights come back.

The concluding chapter of *Taipei Story* is an elegiac coda on a tale of despair. "Forget America. It's not a panacea either," Lon says. "It's just a fleeting hope, giving you a kind of illusion that you can start everything over again." F. Scott Fitzgerald knew about second acts in American life. Lon should have read *Gatsby*. There's a Marilyn Monroe calendar on the wall at Chin's place. Late in the film, a biker waits for Lon, who gets his ass kicked, and then comes back and stabs him. Lon keeps wiping the blood away, as if he doesn't understand what it is. He sits at the roadside where he has been left and won't be found, and in a hallucination watches the Little League World Series play out on a derelict TV.

The overall effect of *Taipei Story* is one of grief. Lon laughs at the dreams that don't matter, which dissipate literally as smoke in the air. It's the transcendent moment in this Yang film—which is all but hauled back to earth by a doctor, seen smoking beside Lon's waiting ambulance, in no particular hurry, since there's nothing left to do.

Back with Mrs. Wei, Chin contemplates the future, now rich in material opportunities but devoid of love. The fractured images that roll with the credits—the cars, glass towers, and movable images of Taipei—form what Leo Chanjen Chen has called a "desolate negative epiphany" (118). Chin has no knowledge of her lover's death, but it doesn't matter. What we have are the reflections of Taipei's skyline, the rushing pictures of traffic streaming across Chin's face, the multiple glass surfaces, the implicit absence of meaning in Lon's demise. Together, they constitute a city of sadness for Edward Yang.

The Terrorizer

Yang's *The Terrorizer* (*Kongbu Fenzi,* 1986) ends with a shot of a novelist vomiting, which would seem to be, among other things, an unsubtle commentary on the process of fiction, Yang's included. But it is also just one more enigmatic element in what is Yang's most difficult, intellectually provocative, and structurally challenging film.

Who is the "terrorizer" of the title? The epithet could refer to several, or all, of the characters. The terrorizer could be the White Chick, for instance, a Eurasian gangster girl we first glimpse dropping out of a window during a police raid, breaking her leg and subsequently collapsing in the street. The actress who plays the White Chick was the catalyst for Yang's making the film in the first place.

In 2001 Yang said,

> I had a lot of things in my head for fifteen, twenty years, which suddenly crystallized in that movie, which was actually one of the fastest I've ever made. The trigger came when someone introduced me to a Eurasian girl who appears in the film and seemed to have potential as an actress. When I started to talk to her, I realized she had all kinds of problems with her mother, who used to lock her up at home. She told me that when she was imprisoned like that, she would avenge herself by making prank phone calls.
>
> "Did you get any fun out of that?" I asked her. Then she said, "Yeah, well one time I did get worried. I rang a number out of the blue, and when a housewife answered the phone, I said: 'I'm your husband's mistress—I want to talk to you.' The line went dead."
>
> I was quite shocked, and thought—that's a time bomb, you could kill people by casually doing that. So then the story came quickly: everything fell together. The narrative is complicated because it shows a range of people who don't have anything to do with each other, and then something so accidental, so arbitrary, as a random phone call brings a severe tragedy to every one of them. ("Taiwan Stories" 134–35)

The White Chick's prank calls to the aforementioned novelist become a crucial factor in the film's central tragedy. But the terrorizer could also be the novelist's husband, who in order to get a promotion lies about a close friend and coworker who is in line for the same job.

Or it might be the novelist herself, whose agonized rewriting of her overdue novel tortures both her and her husband and leads ultimately to that vomitous coda that may or may not supply an answer to one of the film's essential questions: what in the world is going on?

Quite possibly the title refers to fiction itself—or, at least, fiction as perpetrated in the pursuit of selfish aim. The film-concluding upchuck by the character Chou Yu-fen—whose ongoing work of imagination is intrinsically linked with the climactic suicide of her husband—is accompanied by a distinct sense of moral disgust. There is sufficient reason to think Yang is proposing that certain fictions are toxic and therefore corrupt. And there is certainly the suggestion that art is a form of regurgitation, meaning that, in the end, the material in question wasn't really the artist's to begin with.

But most critical evaluations of *The Terrorizer* (sometimes referred to as *The Terrorizers*), understandably, seem to split along what is real and what is not—or what is to be read as "real," at any rate, since the nature of reality versus fiction is what Yang is getting at in the first place. It is also a movie about the *responsibility* of fiction, what we do with what we have, or are, or learn from others. It is a maddeningly oblique movie, until you find the hook. Then, like Yang and his inspiration for making the film, it all comes together quite quickly.

The film has attracted some of the most rigorous analyses in Yang's body of work, including a celebrated essay by Fredric Jameson on the film's importance as a vehicle for the emergence of modern or postmodern impulses in third-world cinema (Jameson 114–57). Chou's imagination, and her ongoing rewrite of her almost completed novel, is the engine for most of what goes on in the movie. It is probably an overstatement to suggest that any or most of the characters—several of whom seem to be blatantly clichéd or fictionally embellished creations and have to be considered as existing on some other level from Chou or her husband, Li Li-chung—are mere figments of her imagination. This despite the fact that Yang is, in only his third full-length feature, making a virtuosically bold, modernist statement about the amorphous nature of fact and fiction—so bold, it seems, that he could hardly provide us any kind of easy explanation for what happens. It might be, for instance, the machinations of the dream state of some tortured Taipei novelist, or even the machinations of some wily Taipei filmmaker. Nothing here is easy, because art isn't either.

Since the earliest days of film, montage theory has been an essential element in the creation of cinematic narrative. Perhaps the most important figures in its development were two Russians. One, Lev Kulishev, joined the Russian State Film School in 1920 and lent his name to the "Kulishev effect," that is, the meaning that the viewer gives a one shot when it is juxtaposed with another. Famous example: show a man's smiling face, then a plate of food. Conclusion: hunger. Show the same man's face and then a beautiful woman. Conclusion: lust. What it means in cinema is that the mind is naturally inclined toward reconciling the unconnected.

The other man behind montage theory was the director and editor Sergei Eisenstein, who in 1925 directed his first feature, *Strike*, and put the Kulishev effect to use. In the years after the October Revolution, he and filmmakers such as Dziga Vertov, in films such as *Potemkin* and *Ivan the Terrible*, not only advanced the art form but explored the capacity of the human intellect. While American films of the period consisted of hundreds of shots, Russian films had thousands, and not just of sequential scenes that clearly advanced a narrative. Through juxtaposition—the sequencing of not-so-clearly related shots—Eisenstein took shot A and shot B and arrived at meaning C.

Eisenstein described himself as an engineer (in his *Diaries* of 1927). Yang, as we have said, was also trained as an engineer, but here the similarity ends, because what Yang attempts in *The Terrorizer* is a virtual dismantling of montage theory.

Opening: Dawn. Car lights penetrate the blackness, colors pierce the eye, sirens assault the ears. "Christ, do you know what time it is?" a man asks a woman. "It's almost daybreak."

"I'll be done soon. Did I bother you?"

She has been reading. Curtains billow in a set of windows, giving us a glimpse of the man's many cameras. The woman is finally asleep. She is not the novelist Chou Yu-fen.

Suddenly, gunshots are fired. There is a view of a body in a street, immovable, evidently (apparently?) dead. Via aerial shots we get a brief glimpse of a man running.

And then a woman awakes, clearly worried—perhaps about the story thus far; perhaps about the man on her apartment terrace, who is doing squat thrusts. It is decidedly disorienting, this shift from an apparent crime scene to a scene of the more domestic variety. But what lends the film its air of peril, or at least uncertainty, is the way Yang establishes the man as distinctly out of place. He could be a client, if the woman had clients. He may just be a visitor; his suit is folded on a chair, as if it were put there the night before by someone without his own closet or any sense of permanence. He puts his shoes on by the door. He could be someone else's husband, clearing out after a one-night stand. But no, in fact, he is Li. And she is Chou Yu-fen.

"Another rewrite?" he responds, when she tells him her plan. "Writing a novel shouldn't be this murderous."

As if fiction is infecting fact, there is real murder—or at least, a body, or an imagined body—on the street. Shooters seem to be in a nearby building (although neither Li nor Chou seems aware of any gunfire; neither is a woman glimpsed cleaning on her terrace, who reacts not at all even as the audience hears the shots). Where are these people? They seem to be in close proximity, but that may be only because of subversive qualities of the montage effect. Yang knows this and exploits it.

Next, we see a cop in sunglasses, doing his impersonation of a character out of *Cool Hand Luke*. He is the only officer who doesn't flinch when more shots go off. He might be imaginary; he's certainly a type. He does, however, direct a scuttling photographer away from the scene. The photographer has crept onto the site to get some pictures and doesn't seem overly concerned by the bullets (although he *is* concerned about the cop). The photographer is evidently experienced at this, but the scene is nonetheless frightening. Even Yang's angles are scary. The cops are oily. They beat a suspect who has fled the house (while the kid snaps his pictures). After leaping from that window, our young White Chick limps away, her leg broken, until she collapses off a curb and into a traffic-snarled street, miraculously never being hit by a car.

Little of this makes sense. How did she get away? The shots were fired from the hell-hole studio apartment, but why do the cops wait until it is empty before blowing it to bits? The SWAT team (or the Taiwanese equivalent) riddles the empty space with bullets, their fusillade an impotent gesture by a morally bankrupt system—or, at least, that might be one theory. Yang is far too subtle and slippery for easy interpretation. But the shot of the Taiwanese cop yawning while the place blows up borders on the burlesque, or a scene out of a Takeshi Kitano film.

Yang cuts to the novelist. What is the distance between the shooting scene and her unfinished novel? Suspicions are that it might be the distance between synapses.

The film then moves to the laboratory of a city hospital, and we have settled back into a simpler "reality." A woman is crying; the already somber atmosphere has been disturbed. The high-ranking administrator of the hospital has died; his surviving colleagues stand around, gossiping and making trite comments ("He really smoked too much"). This is Li's place of employment and he sees the chief's death as an opportunity for advancement. Casting suspicions of fraud on a longtime colleague and friend (and creating a work of fiction himself, of course), he becomes the acting director.

Li's wife, meanwhile, their cold war not improving, decides to move out of their home. Ostensibly, this has to do with the prank phone calls she's been getting, from the White Chick with the broken leg. But she

Cora Miao in *The Terrorizer,* after receiving the phone call.

really is out to resume an old dalliance with a former coworker. "I hear I was in one of your short stories," he comments offhandedly. She is noncommittal. All relationships seem amorphous, because they are built on fictions.

We're shown a window washer clinging to the glass on the outside of the building (a typical Yangian hallucination). Yang makes manga-like images such as this one flash by. The precariousness of the window washer's perch punctuates a scenario based on various betrayals (or, referring to the title, terrors) of friends, mates, a system, a people.

A bartender, on the phone, drops a pregnant comment. "The more crowded a place," he says, "the safer it is." Taipei, for instance? Presumably, the bartender speaks to the White Chick's fugitive boyfriend, but his voice is heard even as the image is relocated to that blown-to-bits apartment. Realities, overlapping like unstable tectonic plates, shift and grate against each other. The photographer and his girlfriend, the all-night reader, split up while we listen to "Smoke Gets in Your Eyes." The mother of the White Chick has a tantrum. We get another incongruous/fantastic image of that window washer, with another man materializing in the window.

What Chou will say is that her world is too small. But is it? Or have the demands of fiction sucked the breath out of her life? She will also say that novels are novels. "No need to mix it up with what actually happened." But Yang is doing just that. And the distance between life and fiction is getting shorter and shorter.

In bed, Chou's boyfriend, looking bored, asks her, with no real interest, "What are you thinking about?"—his ennui suggesting that no one here wants to know anything, if it isn't about them. "He must trust you," he says of her husband, referring to her absence. "No, that's not it," she says, leaving her meaning unspoken but clear enough.

The White Chick is another creation, maybe of Chou's, but she is certainly intended as a symbol of fiction. She's tough—much tougher than the dilettante toughs in the movie. But she is also a creature who might have inhabited one of those manga comic books Yang digested as a teenager. In one scene, she and her old boyfriend—who was arrested at the scene of the opening shootout—run a sex scam at a local hotel. She's caught stealing the mark's wallet, and he takes off his belt with the

Yon Anshuen (left) gets arrested, in
The Terrorizer.

intention of beating her. But she's too quick. Before he can move, she rushes across the entire room and stabs him dead.

How she accomplishes this particular feat might seem somewhat puzzling, given the space and time involved, but not if you have configured your movie—or, at least, a certain scene—as if it were playing out in twin panels of a Japanese comic book (something that differs dramatically from the signature Yangism of letting people enter and leave his frame without allowing the camera to follow them around).

In *The Terrorizer,* as in Yang's other movies, Taipei is cast as a city, much like New York historically, where instant obsolescence rules. As a result, people are constantly shifting relationships, forging new connections, and generally sabotaging what tenuous links they do have with their fellow man or woman. This too generates the terror of the title.

As the critic Peggy Chiao wrote of the film:

Edward Yang has skillfully blended his characters into their urban environment, letting his audience receive the full impact of Taipei's reality and its latent dangers and crises. In this environment, no one can escape the hidden terror because it is normal, as implied in marriages breaking up, the pressures of upward mobility, urban crimes, suicides and violence. The point is well illustrated in the title of Chou Yu-fen's book, *Change Is a Revolving Wheel.* The terror is transferable, as illustrated by the wayward girl's prank calls. All one has to do is open the phone book and call all those listed with the same name as Li Li-chung and any one of them could come to harm. These details cause the audience to look carefully at the organization of the whole plot structure to discover the rich veins linking the scattered scenes and their intentions. (Ou, chap. 4, 30)

There is a self-destructiveness afoot in *Terrorizer* that seems a pathological symptom of societal unrest. Li, for example, has all but torpedoed his marriage (although when he can't find Chou, he panics). He has also screwed over his friend at work, who tells Li, "They're trying to make me the scapegoat," never guessing who set him up. White Chick takes up with our photographer, whom she finds living in her old shot-up apartment. He's decorating one wall with a portrait of her, composed of dozens of Polaroids (it's a thrilling shot), which she watches as a breeze yet again blows in through the curtains (a sure sign from Yang to be cautious about any assumptions you may be making). The photographer has also turned the place into a giant darkroom, blocking out day and night. Which is it, she asks him. Peeking outside, Yang gives us that holy moment between light and dark, casting the entire city into moral dusk; White Chick, after listening to her new paramour's profession of undying love, steals his cameras (although she brings them back a short time later).

"You can't ever understand if you don't by now," Chou says, ostensibly to her husband, but speaking directly to the camera. What is it we don't get? The entire storyline, maybe, which reaches a crescendo of perceptual discord as the film comes to a close. Li, who has never read his wife's books and lies about his home life, is finally given his comeuppance. He is denied the job he wants and is even refused an audience with his boss (who cravenly hides in his office till Li goes away). But he tells his friend, the cop, that he got the job after all. "My hard work was appreciated," he says. "For a man, a successful career is the most important thing. The rest is meaningless"—the rest meaning wife, love,

Li Liqun (right) talks to Cora Miao in the kitchen, in *The Terrorizer*.

honor, respect. But having said this, he has rendered himself meaningless, and he takes the only course left to him.

The cop is interesting here. A novelist's creation,he is totally implausible as a friend of the husband, or of anyone else for that matter. His place in the movie is to provide the source of a gun, which Li then takes on a imaginary shooting spree that ends with a great image of a blasted vase, teetering, leaking water, but not quite collapsing. Li shoots a mirror instead of his wife and winds up dead in the shower, discovered by the cop. Li's last act is a dream and suicide, rather than a homicide.

Chou's novel, which touches on murder, wins her a prize. Yang's prize at this point in his career was the realization that he needed to make his own reality, acknowledging the fallacy that one must draw a hard line between reality and fiction. He also learned that through the elimination of certain elements—explanations, for instance, or sympathetic characters, or any central viewpoint—he could create the sense of alienation and discord that he wanted. It must have been a rough thing with which to come to terms. Look, after all, at the effect it has on Chou.

A Brighter Summer Day

A Brighter Summer Day (*Gulingjie Shaonian Sharen Shijian,* 1991) is a passion play, an elegy, a Wild West show, an Eastern *West Side Story,* and a synthesis and reimagining of everything Yang had done up to its release in 1991. Originally about four hours long (though shown frequently in a version closer to three hours), the film has an angry energy that comes as a surprise after the frank, clinical introduction that appears on the screen:

> Millions of Mainland Chinese fled to Taiwan with the National Government after its civil war defeat by the Chinese Communists in 1949. Their children were brought up in an uneasy atmosphere created by the parents' own uncertainty about the future. Many formed street gangs to search for identity and to strengthen their sense of security.

Through it—appropriately enough, considering the movie's preoccupation with Americana and Western accessories—Yang cuts to the chase.

Based on a shocking real-life story about a Taiwanese schoolgirl's murder, *A Brighter Summer Day* ought to be considered, along with *Yi Yi,* one of the twin pillars of Yang's work to date. It is a movie in which the director refocuses his attention on the same aesthetic techniques and sociological bugaboos that informed his previous films, but with a far more operatic scope and a mournfully trenchant delivery.

A Brighter Summer Day picks the scab off of life in Taiwan in a way Yang's earlier films only seemed to, and it finds an unhealable wound. That the film incited hostility and resentment among blinkered Taiwanese loyalists is understandable, as it questions the soundness, even the existence, of the national soul.

Why open in a film studio, with a troubled movie in noisy rehearsal? Because two of the key characters—the quiet, intelligent S'ir and his kinetic little sidekick, Cat—are hiding on a catwalk two stories up, reading a book or watching the proceedings (their perch makes us think, unavoidably, of the opera-house scene in *Citizen Kane*). What is to unfold is a dramaturg's-eye-view of the melodrama developing—circa September 1960—on the island of Taiwan.

"Why this color?" an unseen actress complains about her dress. "Why worry about color!" the director bellows. "It's a black-and-white film!!"

The film-within-a-film is a production in serious trouble. The aging actress got her role through her "friendship" with someone known only as "the boss." The director resents her for it. This theater, this alleged sphere of art where truth is to be mined, is poisoned by self-interest and resentment. Whether the "theater" or "arena" in question turns out to be politics or education or simply youth, the same theme of systemic corruption surges relentlessly through the film.

As he did in *The Terrorizers,* Yang is taking the line between fiction and reality and giving it a snap. The film studio, though incidental to the principal storyline, will serve as a kind of reflecting pool for other things that go on in the movie—just as *A Brighter Summer Day* itself provides a mirror for Taiwanese dysfunction. The characters, players in their own American-pop-fueled fiction, will move in and out of its frame, just as they move in and out of the arena of respectable life in Taiwan. The studio will also serve as a kind of sanctuary, where S'ir, the "hero" of the film—its tragic hero, its quiet man, its Shane-on-adolescent-hormones—will retreat each of the several times that reality rears its ugly head.

Cat and S'ir drop the book; the director yells; a security guard with a flashlight chases the two, cornering S'ir as Cat makes tracks. "You're not getting away, kid," the old guy says, before adding—like a central-casting Nazi in a bad B-movie—"I have ways of making you talk." But the resourceful Cat chucks a rock through the window, the guard pursues Cat, and S'ir gets away—but not before ducking back in, just to steal the flashlight.

This is kid's stuff, like their friends' fascination with Red Bean, the girl who sells things from a table under the archway at school. "I bet you they're red," one says, meaning her underpants, which they'll steal a look at later.

What Yang will do, however, with increasing severity and tension, is to close the gap between adolescent mischief and full-grown mayhem until there is no gap and everyone is implicated in the most heinous violence, which grows out of almost nothing. Meanwhile, S'ir, as he runs

Edward Yang (left) on the set of a banquet scene in *A Brighter Summer Day.*

from the theater, spots two young lovers kissing in the nearby darkened woods. From such happenstance, planets fall off their axes.

In a *Chicago Reader* article about the key directors of contemporary Iran and Taiwan, the critic Jonathan Rosenbaum wrote that *A Brighter Summer Day,* in its 230-minute version,

> belongs in the company of key works of our era: Kira Muratova's *The Asthenic Syndrome;* Bela Tarr's *Satantango;* [Abbas] Kiarostami's *Close-up, Life and Nothing More,* and *Taste of Cherry;* and Hou [Hsiao-hsien's] trilogy—*City of Sadness, The Puppetmaster,* and *Good Men, Good Women.*
>
> Indeed, Yang's film surpasses these other masterpieces in its novelistic qualities, richly realizing a physical and social world as dense with family, community, and other personal ties as any John Ford film, and furnished with more sheer physical presence (including characters, settings, and objects) than any other fiction film I know of from the 90s. It took Yang four years to prepare—much of the time apparently spent training his superb cast, which is mainly composed of nonprofessionals. In fact, this

film is so uncommonly good that Yang's other very impressive works pale beside it.

This was written before *Yi Yi*, but Rosenbaum was right. *A Brighter Summer Day* is as dense with intersecting characters and plotlines as any novel and, like any major novel, it has to be mapped out before one can go much further.

Picking up a thread that ran through *Taipei Story, A Brighter Summer Day* is an autopsy of generational conflict. S'ir's parents, Shanghai intellectuals who lost almost everything in their flight to Taiwan, suffer a dislocation and disenchantment that cripple them as parents. We get an ironically Ozu-level view of their home life in one early scene. It is morning. Family members are going to school, to work; a daughter loses a button; Mom loses her patience. Dad walks around useless. The perspective is almost at floor level, which turns out to be S'ir's point of view: having just roused himself from sleep, he watches the morning melee from what is basically a cupboard, which lies beside that of his brother. The impression we get is that the kids have been put in storage by parents who simply cannot cope. (One of the cuts that Yang imposed on the film, to shorten it in order to get distribution, occurs just at the end of this one take. When S'ir arrives in the kitchen, it's a different day. It is smooth editing but ultimately bewildering.)

The mother is particularly disaffected. When S'ir tells her his eyesight is blurry, she offers a dismissive "Get to bed earlier." The eyesight question comes up again, as she and Dad return home from a party, where Dad has had a fateful meeting with Mr. Wang (more about him later). Preoccupied with the documentation problem that is preventing her from resuming her teaching career, Mom treats S'ir's complaint as a relatively insignificant irritation. "I hope we can avoid buying him glasses," she says. He should, instead, take the free shots offered at school.

It is unclear whether the shots she has in mind are an antidote to some epidemic of blurry eyesight affecting Taiwan as a whole, but it is when the school nurse is giving S'ir his dose that he first catches sight of Ming, one of the more fascinating characters in Yang's entire filmography.

We see Ming through a doorway, Yang's usual key when something revelatory is being brought to the fore or a character is being isolated (and our focus along with it). She has injured her ankle. How she has done it will be significant, too; no reaction in this film results from an insignificant action. Her injury is being tended by a young doctor who will later play an important role in her life. Unlike like every other adult in the film, he holds young people—certain young people at least—in something other than contempt.

Yang uses the first meeting of S'ir and Ming to lighten the tone. Told to help Ming back to class, S'ir doesn't really help her; he sort of percolates along beside her, teasingly, speeding up, slowing down. Were he a peacock, his tail feathers would be on full alert.

The two elude a school officer and hide for a while. "We can't stay here forever," Ming says, and you can't help wondering if she is talking about the two of them or if she is articulating the conclusion of an entire generation whose only home, Taiwan, has been treated by their parents with utter contempt.

Ming is the girlfriend of Honey, another essential figure, and a fascinating one, who is on the run from the law for having killed a rival gang leader—possibly over Ming. Although Ming travels from boy to

Lisa Yang (left) and Zhang Zhen, in *A Brighter Summer Day.*

boy like a starving gamine at a smorgasbord, it is a hunger for security, not sex, she is trying to sate. Ming is fatherless (like so many characters in Yang's films), and her mother is an asthmatic who works as a domestic but loses jobs regularly because of her illness. The mother's employers are meanhearted and mean; the first one we meet tries to get a discount from the doctor mentioned above. An uncle with whom Ming's family will move in (he is their only relative) provides the voice of a distemperate and bitterly oppressive, middle-aged middle class. "I tell you, I *am* the country," he roars. "When I was her age, I was fighting the Japs and the Commies."

Likewise, Mr. Wang, the center of attention at the party S'ir's parents attend, brings up the Commies. He has been to America—"It's great! Mickey Mouse! Disneyland!" He has also been to an A-bomb plant. "If I were an expert," he says, "I could have learned to make my own atom bomb—then I could blow the Commies to hell."

More important is his heart-to-heart with S'ir's father. "Make long-term plans while there's still time," Wang advises him. "Throw away your old Shanghai intellectual mentality. Be more flexible."

"I'm helping you," he says, "so you'll help me," articulating the gang mentality, taken off the street and into the corridors of power.

But is Ming supposed to care? Is any young person on Taiwan? What she would like is some protection, a modicum of respect, a little security, a home that doesn't move—unlike the island itself, which is a shape-shifting atoll for its uneasy occupants. The boys of *A Brighter Summer Day* are seduced by gang life because it offers the same kind of solace Ming is seeking through men. Their recourse is seen as romantic; hers, as the equivalent of prostitution.

That she, and Yang, understands so well the irony of all this gives an enormous poignancy to Ming's relationships—with S'ir, of course, but particularly with Honey. He is the leader, in absentia, of the Little Park Boys (gang names correlate with neighborhoods), to which a number of S'ir's classmates belong, including Sly, S'ir's antagonist. Sly is the figure S'ir spotted in the woods getting a kiss from Ming, although no one knows at this point who was who.

Sly is a vicious, amoral little operator who introduces himself to S'ir by trying to copy his answers on a test. (The competition at school is somewhat ironic, since all the pupils are night students, making them second-class already.) In a postexam confrontation, Sly slaps S'ir and S'ir picks up a baseball bat—the first of many imported Americanisms. He is quite ready to use it, before the dean shows up and gestures for the bat.

The dean, like virtually all authority figures in *A Brighter Summer Day,* is a miserable despot. He clashes with S'ir's father in one of the film's truly pivotal moments. His treatment of S'ir—who has intentionally put a wrong answer on a test, just to trip up Sly—is injustice personified. Merely by defending himself, S'ir is accused of being rude to his teachers. His father fairly explodes. "There's no justice! How can you teach with such a bureaucratic attitude!?" He makes an enemy of the dean, and it will come back to haunt both him and his son.

What follows is the first of two scenes that more or less bookend the film, showing father and son walking their bikes home from the school. The contrast between the two sequences—the first of a father righteous and livid, the second of a shattered man—is certainly among the film's more horrifying dualities. "If a person will apologize for the things he didn't do," father tells son, "then he's capable of doing anything terrible." Dad will be terrorized in a government grilling, forced to fabricate charges against himself and implicate acquaintances in a conspiracy whose nature he doesn't even understand. His indignation with the dean becomes more pitiable with each viewing of the film.

S'ir already knows the world is unjust. Dad is a bit more naive. "You must know that your future can be decided by your own hard work," he tells S'ir, which is, of course, the height of irony in the realm of *A Brighter Summer Day.*

For a while, however, S'ir maintains a certain stature. "Don't think of him as just another good student," Cat tells Sly, in a classically backhanded compliment. "If you lock horns with him, he doesn't fuck around." Neither does Sly. In the gang fight that kicks off the film, Sly rather casually slams a brick into the head of a very small, very young captive from the rival 217 Village, causing a low moan, along with a ribbon of blood, to unfurl from his whimpering victim's mouth. "Never fuck with the Little Park Boys," Sly says, with all the bravado of a guy backed up by a gang, and a brick.

So we have S'ir, Cat, Ming, Sly, and Honey (who will show up later), and these are just the leads. Seemingly tangential but essential are

Threads and S'ir's brother, Lao Er (which means "Prick"), who visit the poolroom headquarters of the 217 gang, put on a display of expertise, and wind up getting taken for a large amount of money. Although this part of the film seems baroque in its intersecting complications, it is also indispensable to the storyline. The poolroom scenario compromises Threads. Along with Sly, who is already compromised because of his dalliance with Ming, Threads is involved in organizing the central event of the film, the concert at the high school.

Staged like an *American Bandstand* episode, the concert is much anticipated, a major sociocultural to-do. The headliners will be a hilarious quartet of Asian rockers, proto-Elvis impersonators who evoke the same kind of squealing response that might have greeted the real thing (copycat culture, Yang suggests, being more than adequate for this crowd). Also on the bill will be Cat, whom we have already heard singing, in his angelic voice, phonetic translations of American pop hits ("Angel Baby," for one). Deuce, who is involved in producing the show, is also going to sing.

But Deuce is more than a little pissed off. During a preconcert huddle, he wants to know why Sly is cutting in on his concert action. He claims that Threads is getting too big a cut. He makes a move. A fight breaks out. Jade, another girl, is in the middle—in more ways than one.

On the sidelines, S'ir speculates about what is going on. The oh-so-wise Cat tells him. "You started it."

"I never said it was Jade," S'ir replies, referring to the mysterious kiss.

"Who else could it be?" counters Cat.

Even Jade says it was she ("It was me"), kissing in the woods with Sly. But of course it wasn't. She is covering for Ming, saving her from the dreaded wrath of Honey.

Amidst the more soap-operatic aspects of *A Brighter Summer Day* and the film's big-novel storyline, Yang is making a film-as-organism. His use of the frame suggests an attempt to impose order on the life he is portraying, just as his camera occasionally backs off or holds still as characters move in and out of its range. The stasis of that range seems to suggest frustration with a life that will not conform to what people, the director included, want it to. Darkness—particularly the deadly blackness in which the 217 slaughter scene is enacted, with murderous bodies moving across a single glaring light—is a character itself in *A Brighter Summer Day.* It is as inescapable as the angst that infects the souls of its inhabitants.

That most of the boys have nicknames—Airplane, Cat, Sly, Panty, Honey, Deuce, Blind Man—is significant, particularly in regard to S'ir's relationship to Honey, with whom he shares outsider status. Honey has a nickname and S'ir doesn't, which is a clue that the latter is even further outside the main—or soon will be—than Honey, the fugitive killer.

A kind of sailor-suited Harry Lime, the memorable villain from *The Third Man,* Honey is pure cinema—handsome, charming, doomed. His outfit makes him look like the little guy on the Cracker Jack box, and so does his physical attitude. But he manages to pull it off. While on the lam and holing up with friends, he had nothing to do but read. So he read. "I was reading ten swordsman novels a day," he tells S'ir. "Then I told them to rent the thickest books they could find. I found that people in the past were just like us street gangs." He read *War and Peace,* although he can't remember the title.

"If you'd written back," S'ir tells Honey, referring to the letters he received from Ming, "none of this would have happened," meaning Ming's dalliances with S'ir, Sly, and Tiger—yet one more lover—with whom she sprained her ankle, a giveaway of guilt. (In *A Brighter Summer Day,* everything interconnects.)

"Shit," Honey says, "if I could write I'd write a novel, one that guys like me could read in the future.

"It's too late," he adds. "I didn't study hard enough." Honey is not just pure cinema, he is pure regret. But he has got something S'ir doesn't have: introspection. He couldn't have read *War and Peace* and not come away with something. The viewer can't help thinking about the unspoken title and what it means to Yang's world.

Conversely, we have Ma—the son of a general, and a newcomer rumored to have hacked up an adversary with a samurai sword (recovered Japanese weapons, found in attics and other out-of-the-way places, play a large part in *A Brighter Summer Day* and further symbolize the island's reliance on borrowed culture). Ma is yet another character integral to the film, and he is easily the most privileged, affluent kid in the picture (Ming's mother will go to work for him at one point late in the movie).

His presence is enough to scare off a group of gang members who drag S'ir out of class one night (while in a hilarious ancillary shot, S'ir's little friends break up their desk chairs to make cudgels and then set out to rescue him). Ma becomes an important ally of S'ir, until clashing with him over their differing attitude toward girls.

What Ma represents seems fairly obvious: the triumph of violence, embodied in his father's status and influence and in Ma's ability to behave sociopathically without answering for anything. Taiwan's history of bloodshed obscures its morality, the film is saying, and the respect shown to Ma means that no one can see the truth. Ma may be the most heinous of all Yang's characters.

S'ir, for his part, is merely blind about Ming, or rather blind to her circumstances, and occupies whatever vacancy exists between Emil Jannings in *The Blue Angel* and Leslie Howard in *Of Human Bondage.* ("I'm like this world," she tells S'ir. "I'll never change.") Ma is different. He and S'ir double date with Jade and a girlfriend, and the foursome goes to see *Rio Lobo*—in which the pop star Ricky Nelson echoes the music heard at the school concert, thus bringing things full circle. S'ir has less luck with his date than Ma does. So Ma makes a gesture of friendship:

Zhang Zhen getting harassed, in *A Brighter Summer Day.*

"Go on, take Jade," he tells S'ir, who follows her across the schoolyard and into one of Yang's hallucinatory reveries: Jade, twirling about, spins around and then a train screams by in a cut that drops the film into the next day. It happens in a flash, and it is delirious. It suggests a wish, on Jade's part, to simply transcend the entire sordid world.

It is startling too because so much of *A Brighter Summer Day* takes place in the dark. The 217 gang's poolroom can't keep its lights lit; the initiation-night slaughter takes place mostly against an inky black, and when S'ir and Ming visit the studio again, the light stretches in through the opening doors like a sleepy cat.

Ming has been asked to take a screen test by that director, who is sick of his actress (he tells the older woman, "This role needs a teenager. You're forty and don't look a day younger"). While at the studio with Ming, S'ir admits that he is afraid of Honey. She laughs, and he asks why. "I'm laughing at how honest you are. People like you always get burned." Honey, she says, is a really honest person, too. The problem is that when he sees something wrong, he wants to change it. "He wants to change the world." Yang's analogy: a desire for change makes one an outlaw or worse.

It is a virtual Nicholas Ray moment when Honey arrives, like James Dean, at the school concert. That the kids dress so properly, so naively, and behave so decorously is just one of the many incongruities Yang sets up. The kids also stand, very solemnly, for the national anthem; outside the building itself, the 217 gang's enforcer, Shandong, tells the kids to straighten up for the song—and they do. But not Honey, who is totally outside life. To his nemesis, Shandong, he later says, "Only two types of people scare me. Those who aren't afraid to die, and those who know no shame. Which kind are you?" Shandong promptly pushes him in front of a speeding car.

Honey's death accelerates the action. Ming grows closer to S'ir, who becomes almost giddy in his happiness with her. S'ir's father, meanwhile, is arrested one night and taken to an anonymous government office for interrogation; "Just write what you feel," he is told, as if it is an artistic exercise. Resistant at first, Dad eventually gets the point, which is to implicate whomever the interrogator wants him to. Broken, he writes furiously, and at length, and then is summarily dismissed. Nothing mattered in the end. He is left with no self-respect, no courage, and no pride. And that was precisely the point.

The father disintegrates, rousing the family in the middle of the night to check for intruders and beating S'ir's brother viciously over a missing watch. Meanwhile S'ir has a parallel meltdown. Ming has become close to Ma, who better fits her objectives. S'ir's reaction is bitter and antisocial. In one penetrating bit of Yang framing, S'ir comes to Ma's house to force a confrontation, and we watch it entirely from inside Ma's house; S'ir never crosses the threshold. It is another Yang doorway shot, but at this point S'ir is not only completely outside the main, he is even outside of the movie.

He is further outside, even, than Honey was. Honey, not brilliant but smart enough to absorb the lessons of literature, was self-taught and self-recriminating; S'ir, sharply intelligent but the product of a cripplingly bureaucratic education system, can't even access the qualities he needs to save himself, from himself.

You might say that S'ir's murder of Ming at the end of *A Brighter Summer Day* is the film's climax, and you would have made a pun. S'ir's pent-up excitement, ardor, and ultimately anger put the entirety of the film in a sexual context, a very teenaged, hormonal-delirium sexual context in which mad things happen that no one can explain. "How can you make a film when you can't even tell real from fake?" S'ir screams at the film director, when asked about Ming during his last trip inside the studio. How indeed? S'ir's assumption that art requires truth is a final, poignant exclamation point on his shattered innocence and abandonment.

A Brighter Summer Day is a cautionary tale and an indictment, not of S'ir but of the callously indifferent atmosphere in which Yang saw Taiwanese children being brought up. When Cat is rebuffed while trying to visit S'ir in prison, he leaves behind a tape recording of the Elvis song he has sung. "What's that?" one guard asks after Cat walks away. "Shit," his partner says, tossing the cassette into the garbage. He hates Cat, it seems, not just because he has what the older man wants (time), or what he has lost (hope), but because there is always a chance the boy, and Taiwanese youth in general, won't turn out like him. So he does what he can to make things right.

A Confucian Confusion

> Confucius: The city is too crowded
> Disciples: What can we do about it?
> Confucius: Make the people rich.
> Disciples: What comes next, after they are made rich?
> Two thousand years of poverty and struggles later, it took a city named Taipei just twenty years to become one of the wealthiest cities in the world.
>
> —Introductory titles to *A Confucian Confusion*

> The situation in all of Asia is terrible now. It's not an economic problem, it's not a financial problem, it's not a political problem, it's a serious cultural problem. *A Confucian Confusion* is the first and so far only attempt at self-reflection: at examining what is wrong with trying to head into the twenty-first century with a fourth-century B.C. ideology.
>
> —Edward Yang, Chicago, 1997

It was one of those Edward Yang–like coincidences. While I was watching *A Confucian Confusion* (*Duli Shidai*, 1994) again a couple of years ago, the news was breaking about the pop singer Mariah Carey's astounding separation agreement with her recording company, EMI, which planned to pay her $28 million in exchange for dropping her $80 million contract. Like a farmer on a subsidy, she would be paid big bucks, as long as she did not make any records. Considering the effect of *A Confucian Confusion*'s dire (and very funny) portrayal of corporations, popular artists, and the meager gap between them, it was one of those moments of optimism mixed with the blues.

In *A Confucian Confusion,* Yang's take on the machinations of pop culture achieves Himalayan heights of cynicism, about either public taste (or lack thereof) or the motivations of self-described (especially self-described) "artists" and the equally cynical way that consumers of entertainment are perceived by those who entertain them. So the Carey news came across like a late summer breeze. Sure, the economy was in a bind. No, record companies didn't have money to spend marketing a product that wouldn't sell anyway, at least not in the numbers that such a contract required. And Carey had recently executed one of the louder flops in the history of movie debuts (*Glitter*).

And yet, somehow, some way, the obscene remuneration of mediocre performers, the phenomenon of artist-as-media-creation, the banal-ization of the once-great American art form of the popular song—was all that beginning to come to an end?

As Yang might say, nah.

"Life, plays, what's the difference?" the director/playwright/self-described artist Birdy asks in *A Confucian Confusion,* roller-skating around his office full of journalists. "Popular personalities open doors, popular plays sell tickets. My ideal is to create popular plays that sell a lot of tickets."

"Is this your first comedy?"

"Right!"

"You were into postmodern abstraction before. Why have you changed?"

"An artist must reflect reality," Birdy says. "If you think Taipei is a postmodern comedy [that] you don't understand—that's your problem!"

"Why are you doing comedy now?"

"Because I am an optimist. Everyone's having a good time. Why spoil it?"

Birdy's bubble was the seemingly unpoppable Asian economic boom of the mid-nineties, which Asia discovered could, in fact, evaporate like a soft, wet kiss. So *A Confucian Confusion* is a movie of a very specific moment. At the same time, Yang's first comedy (like Birdy's) is frequently hilarious, if subtly so, and deals with what happens when the affairs of the heart are dictated by the marketplace.

"You know what I would want to be if I weren't an artist?" Birdy asks his media inquisitors. "A politician. Box office is most democratic. Buying a ticket is like voting. My ultimate political belief is in equality."

"What's equality?" someone asks

"When everyone thinks the same."

Birdy may be an asshole, but his attitude is still a fairly accurate reflection of boom-time philistinism and a belief in mass taste as morally correct. When the issue of intellectual property rights comes up, which certainly seems a moral issue in and of itself, Birdy is almost apoplectic, and not because of any remorse. He has ripped off an early novel by the once-successful husband of the woman we'll call Sister, the otherwise unidentified sibling of Molly, whose "culture company" is involved in music, television, advertising, books, and the production of Sister's television talk show (in which she plays the world's romantic advisor). "Relax," she tells Birdy. "People are just jealous of success." One can almost hear Yang hissing with artistic outrage.

A Confucian Confusion may not be Yang's best movie in terms of structure or pacing (it does bog down), but it is a movie rife with ideas about the corruption of culture, the way in which money creates, buys, and sells "art," and the way various kinds of corruption cause various kinds of corruption. It is also very droll, although the comedy is delivered in such deadpan fashion it is understandable if the jokes get lost.

Take Sister, who one day has Birdy on her show.

"For publicity, artists will try anything to be different," a smiling Sister says over the air. "They propagate sex and violence like venereal disease. They paint our society with exaggerated pessimism. They turn a sunny word, ART, into a ghastly word like AIDS.

"Luckily," she chirps, "the sun always shines on our marriages and our emotional health."

Considering what happens in *A Confucian Confusion,* that last line should bring down the house. If it doesn't, it's partly because even the biggest frauds in the movie take themselves totally seriously, while the genuinely sincere people are wracked by doubt—Yang's definition, it soon becomes clear, of what sincerity really means: the arrival at moral truth by entertaining other people's points of view.

Jumping around a bit, chronologically, we might note that the title of the movie is also the title of the new book by Sister's estranged husband—who began years before as a romantic writer and the idol of teenage girls everywhere but has evolved into the Knut Hamsun of Far East Asia. ("I told him his recent work was too serious to sell," Molly says, "and he got mad.") In the husband's novel, Confucius returns after twenty-five hundred years to see what kind of world his legacy is responsible for. He is greeted everywhere as a rousing success, but only because his entire life's work is applauded as history's greatest put-on. When he tries to explain himself, his explanation is perceived as a put-on, too. Eventually, his enemies destroy him with rumors.

Yang punctuates the film with italicized chapter-type headings, the first of which—*She Sports That Pair of Dimples and Everyone Adores Her*—refers to Qiqi, the extremely pretty aide to Molly. Qiqi's sweetness of both smile and disposition is seen by some in the film—and, more important, by some outside the film, too—as a fraud. What we begin to perceive as an audience, however, is that Qiqi herself is worried, because she fears that people think she's faking, or perhaps because maybe she really is.

In *A Brighter Summer Day*, the character S'ir berates the film director for wanting to cast his devious girlfriend in one of his movies. "How can you make a film," S'ir yells, "when you can't even tell real from fake?" It's the same at the heart of *A Confucian Confusion*. Like the Author's resurrected Confucius, Qiqi is victimized by a society that can't tell the genuine from the counterfeit (another chapter heading reads, *When Fakes Are More Real Than the Real*). On one hand, she is irresistible. On the other, people in Yang's Taipei have become suspicious of that which has become foreign, such as taste, decency, or a smiling face that isn't masking calculation. The result is the slaughter of innocence.

Trying to coerce a coworker into staying on after Molly has trimmed the man's staff (the firm is in trouble), Qiqi declares, with all honesty, "We're all emotionally connected here." "Don't you think emotions are dangerous nowadays?" the worker answers, adding that even Qiqi's multiple charms—her "innocence, loveliness, tenderness, vivacity"—can all be faked. At this point Larry, the biggest faker on the company payroll, shows up. "I love your innocence, loveliness, tenderness, vivacity," he tells her. If Qiqi is not suffering self-doubt at this point, she certainly should be.

Larry, who is a friend of Akeem—Molly's fiancé and the money man behind her company—sits down with Molly in her office, which looks out across the spired plain of downtown Taipei. "Our society rests on common values," he says. He maintains that it is the *emotional factor*—something he seems to have conceived of as a kind of cultural Prozac—that separates the Chinese from the rest of the world, and it is the thing that, if you can market it, serves as the key to success. It is also the Chinese social lubricant. "Western folks are too rigid and legal-minded, so they all need psychiatrists," he says and then compares friendships to investments.

"When I was reading your financial statements I was moved," Larry tells Molly, "because I read from them your innermost passions." Molly just stares (which is one reason we like her).

Qiqi would have been a "perfect cultural product," Larry says to Molly. Why? "The very sight of her makes people comfortable." Larry's so-called *emotional factor* is the reductio ad absurdum of pop-culture pandering.

Qiqi is engaged to Ming (a male Ming), but among the various couples in *A Confucian Confusion*, they are totally wrong for each other. Scratch that: *all* the couples are wrong for each other. How they rationalize their relationships—Molly's with Akeem, for instance, which seems based solely on his ability to fund her firm—points up Yang's bewilderment with the sway of money.

Ming, for instance, is a militant conformist—essentially a coward in his conservatism, albeit a coward with a heart. When a contractor who is seriously behind schedule and liable for fines arrives at his home, literally with babe in arms and begging for a reprieve, Ming can mount no resistance. His coworker Liren, however, can.

"He's bankrupt," Liren says, "so he's useless. You think we're crusaders?" Liren will in fact agree to fudge the paperwork and get the contractor off the hook, but he will get fired for it, while Ming simultaneously is recognized for his "talent." What talent? A talent for being invisible.

"What's wrong with being like the others?" he asks Liren.

"To be like the others," he is told, "is the easiest way to avoid responsibility."

"I have a steady job because I don't complain," Ming tells Qiqi. What Ming aspires to is a kind of lofty mediocrity—which to Yang is the prime product of a society devoted solely to material gain.

The schematic of *A Confucian Confusion* is sort of a triangle within a wheel, and, in keeping with Yang's affinity for young women, three such women stand at the corners of that triangle. One, of course, is Qiqi, whose beauty belies her true sweetness. "You think that smile works every time?" the Author asks her, when she tries to get him to sign a release for Birdy. The hardness that overcomes Qiqi over the course of the movie, however marginal, is the result of people's being blind to the truth; actually *being* innocent, or lovely or tender or vivacious, is asking for trouble.

Merely acting that way, however, is another story. At another point of the triangle is Feng, an actress and the movie's ultimate operator. She gets a job at Molly's company through Larry, because she is sleeping with him. (Molly catches one glance exchanged between them and alerts Qiqi: "Tell her she's fired." This is another reason we like her.)

Feng is Qiqi's antithesis, someone whose very inconstancy possesses a kind of integrity and even a consistency. She is whip smart and calculating, beautiful and dangerous. When she greets Larry at her apartment (having shoved Ming, whom she has just invited up, into a cab), she cautions him about just what would happen to him should he try to get over on Molly. "She'll trap you in her car and start grilling you about me. Then she'd get pissed off and kick you out." This is precisely what Molly has just done. Larry looks stunned but not necessarily any wiser about Feng.

How to keep Molly from telling Akeem that Larry tried to seduce her, and thus derailing Larry's every scheme? "You have to start a sex scandal about her." Feng is Machiavelli-as-supermodel.

Molly, the third in this triumvirate, obviously lies somewhere between Feng and Qiqi. We like her, because she is a no-nonsense person and seems to want to do something serious with her company to promote the arts—despite the drivel (like her sister's show) that makes the serious money. She dresses informally despite her wealthy upbringing (her sister, a clothes horse, has a look that makes her seem old enough to be Molly's mother). If it weren't for the Akeem situation—he being a stupid boor—she would be a font of sincerity.

But Akeem is her Achilles heel, in more ways than she even suspects. Following an initially confusing chapter heading (*The "Feed-Her-to-Death" Policy: A Feast That Starves*), we get a peek at the true nature of both Akeem and his cohort Larry.

Akeem is vomiting into a plant stand, having gotten drunk at a local brothel because of a rumor he heard while away on business ("All China is talking about Molly having an affair," he says. "Talk about a loss of face"). Larry, who has been shot down by Molly in his pathetic attempt to seduce her, talks to Akeem about cutting his losses.

"Remember our master plan," he says. "We feed her what she wants until her stomach hurts. We've fed her ego and starved her brain"— Akeem gave her the culture company as an engagement present, it

Akeem (played by Wang Bosen) contemplates the future amongst traditions, in *A Confucian Confusion*.

seems—"Now the company's a mess. If you pull out now," he says, "no one can blame you. That kills all her excuses for being independent. Sentence her to life."

"Sounds like one of those dissidents," Akeem says, through vomitous lips.

"She even made passes at me!" Larry says. There is no depth, it is clear, to which he won't stoop.

And that is a bit unusual, because throughout *A Confucian Confusion*—and, for that matter, throughout Yang's work—there is very little that is ever morally black or white. Ethics, as it were, is mostly the assortment of gray areas that constitute reality, and although the scheming against Molly by Larry and Akeem is unforgivable on its face, they too are creatures of their environment.

Feng, however, is another story. Everyone in *A Confucian Confusion* is an actor, but Feng in many ways is a real artist. She is utterly convincing, at least to every man she meets; that she suddenly does cartwheels down an alleyway as part of her come-on to Ming is the perfect gesture in the perfect place. We can tell that Ming is transfixed, even though we see only the back of his head (something little Yang-Yang in *Yi Yi* would appreciate). More to the point, Feng is single-minded in her pursuit of what she wants; the goal may in itself be a little vague, but her determination is not.

But what is Yang's view of art and its practitioners? Those who claim to be artists in *A Confucian Confusion,* like Birdy, are frauds. Feng is a fraud, but duplicity is her metier. Birdy will eventually decide that he wants to go into politics ("Art is too much of a hassle") and Akeem decides he might like trying his hand at art; why not, everyone else is. But the film's sympathies lie not in the emotional outer boroughs where artists dwell but in the thick of life, where people like Molly and Qiqi try to live in a way that they can sleep at night. Even the Author, who may be the most aesthetically principled of all the characters (and is our apparent Yang manqué), is as self-absorbed as any outsized narcissist in the movie. It is essential to an understanding of both the movie and Yang—and makes perfect sense—that it is life, not art, that the movie

Qiqi and Molly (right) have an intimate moment
by Molly's pool, in *A Confucian Confusion.*

most fiercely upholds. In fact, had Yang made an artist his hero, in this film at least, it would have been an act of pure hypocrisy.

It is notable that the self-glorification that constitutes so much of contemporary filmmaking is so refreshingly absent from Yang's films generally. One cannot imagine him making a movie about making a movie (although the difficulties he has faced would probably make for one of the better entries in that navel-gazing genre). As the critic Manohla Dargis once wrote, "He loves his characters more than his own extraordinary artistry." And he loves life more than art.

There are gradations of art as well as morality in *A Confucian Confusion*, and varying degrees of security. Molly, obviously, has the confidence of someone born to money. "If Akeem hadn't financed the company, my father would have," she says at one point, although she still defends her engagement to Akeem. Ming, on the other hand, finds his sense of place in a full-throated endorsement of Taipei avarice.

If not for prosperity, he tells Qiqi, "We'd still be arming to 'Recover the Mainland.'" His father, for whom he holds distinctly ambiguous feelings, did prison time for crimes he committed while he was in the finance ministry. His parents, long divorced, constitute poles of his life and they provide his main audience as one of the movie's grand actors. His mother tells him he should visit his father; Ming answers no, that "he never cared about us," even though he has just returned from dinner with his father, the father's second wife, and Qiqi, through whom "Second Auntie" has found a new job. Ming is fooling everyone—maybe—but no one as much as himself.

"Jump the boat before you go down in it," Ming tells Qiqi. But QiQi is loyal to Molly; at least we think she is. As in a David Mamet movie (the ones that postdate *A Confucian Confusion*), the double-dealing comes so fast and thick you begin to doubt your own judgment about which character is sincere and which isn't, just as Qiqi doubts herself.

Doubt affects Yang, too, it seems. In *A Brighter Summer Day*, as noted earlier, there is a moment when the young, promiscuous Jade spins around in a dance and her movement abruptly turns into a fast-moving train; in *Yi Yi*, Yang-Yang has his artistic epiphany watching his love object cross the beam of a movie projector. In *A Confucian Confusion*, the closest Yang comes to giving us one of those transcendental moments is when Feng enters Birdy's studio—they would have been a good match—and walks along the length of it, appearing and disappearing like an apparition behind a streamer of red, which crosses from one end of the room to the other.

In Yang's other films, these semi-hallucinatory moments constituted the arrival of knowledge or beauty. Here, it marks the arrival of acknowledged self-interest and beauty as arch manipulators.

But there is another rather lovely moment. It comes after all the slapstick capers involving the more ridiculous characters (Akeem screaming "Bite my ass!!!" as he chases after Birdy, who he thinks has slept with Molly) and the self-deluded pronouncements of other foolish characters ("My ratings prove that the public appreciates my integrity," Sister tells Molly, while trying to keep the rumors of her marital separation a secret). The moment comes in the darkened room at the Author's apartment, where Qiqi, despondent over the ostensible pointlessness of her life and its attendant anxieties, has taken refuge with his books. Sister arrives to talk things out with the Author. Within the almost sepia-toned bedroom, with its wandering shadows and fugitive memories, they almost make it clear why they ever married to begin with. These two individuals, who couldn't be more different in what they value—she, the approval of the unwashed and uneducated; he, the approval of himself—were once in love and devoted. Vestiges of affection float like whispers through the gray light, evoking the indistinct and amorphous moorings of each life in this movie, which, for all its low comedy and high dudgeon, is really about lone, lost people.

A Confucian Confusion really rattles around both the city and the sense of Taipei, perhaps rightly. A tautly constructed comedy about the state of mind Yang found there in the early nineties would have been a misrepresentation or certainly would have ended up being more about comedy than about the city's soul. There is a lot that is really funny about the film—Ming's uncle's obsession with the NBA, for instance, or Ming's first encounter with Feng (Ming: "Don't be sad." Feng: "I lost my contact lens"). Other bits are more mildly amusing, such as the cell-phone fixations or the fact that everyone eats at TGI Fridays. In its scattered and perhaps even frenzied way, *A Confucian Confusion* captures something that might not be timeless (Mariah Carey might not write a song about it). But then, would we want it to be?

Liren (left, played by Chen Yiwen) and Ming (Wang Yeming) have a drink after work during a satellite broadcast of a championship NBA game, in *A Confucian Confusion*.

In the press book to *A Confucian Confusion*, Yang wrote the following:

> Like all the books on Chinese history we studied, over 2,500 years' worth, and most of the recent Chinese-language films that depict the past, poverty and sufferings are central themes. Wealth was never really intended for the people in Confucian doctrines, which enforced more than anything else the central authority's legitimacy with rigid

social structures coated with moral justifications to stress conformism, discipline, and personal sacrifices for social harmony and group security. Ironically, this conformism and discipline bore fruit to all these countries in their economic miracles and double-digit annual growths of the past two decades. Suddenly, as a result, we find ourselves in a position where we have run out of Confucian teachings, as well as Western solutions such as Democracy, from which to model ourselves. We may know how to tell the world what to do, as with the human rights issues, but do we know how to tell ourselves what to do for our own future? This confusion has created ever threatening anxieties in all the details of our daily lives.

Mahjong

Although it features a bloody murder, double suicide, brutal beatings, gang banging, and a rather bitter take on Taipei as a repository of Euro-trash, *Mahjong* (*Majiang*, 1996) is a comedy, one of two among Yang's feature films. Along with *A Confucian Confusion,* which it follows chronologically, *Mahjong* is a not-so-straight social satire, setting it apart from Yang's multicharacter social epics (*A Brighter Summer Day, Yi Yi*) and the earlier, more obscurist and Antonioni-influenced exercises in character and alienation (*That Day, on the Beach, Taipei Story*). It also qualifies, nearly, as an English-language movie.

"Winston Chen is missing," read the opening subtitles, which also tell us that Chen's debts have spiraled out of control and that the underworld is after him. If the mobsters can't get him—which they can't—they will get to him through his son.

Chen's heir, the almost totally charmless Red Fish Chen, is a middle-class hustler, a budding gangster who is following in his father's footsteps by carrying a gun and running small-time scams on local characters (Jay, for instance, the screamingly gay owner of a local hair salon and habitué of the nightclub where *Mahjong* gets started). Tooling around Taipei in a truck with one of his posse, Red Fish is unaware of being followed by a motor scooter carrying one of the local mob soldiers who are assigned to find Red Fish, in order to find his father. The two in the truck are out to smash Jay's pink Mercedes and convince him—as per the "prediction" of their friend and faux shaman, Little Buddha—that the car's number was up. Contributions, they think, will then be forthcoming.

The mobster (who, quite comically, reports to his bosses via cell phone) sees them suddenly swerve and smash into the car and doesn't know what to think.

But we do, at least about the world Yang is setting up, a mid-nineties demimonde of imported hustlers, upwardly mobile prostitutes, socio-pathic teenagers, and one lone innocent named Marthe (played by the French starlet Virginie Ledoyen), who has come in search of Markus (Nick Erickson), a Brit without portfolio and the tall drink of poisonous water who left her pregnant in Paris. Yang's portrait is of city-as-magnet for the detritus of a flourishing world economy ("Rejects from their own stinking countries," as Jay calls them) who come to Taipei in search of easy money.

Besides Markus, who is dating the wealthy but profoundly stupid and needy Allison ("If not for Allison's family money, he'd still be on a bread line in London," Jay says of Markus), there is Ginger (the hope-less Diana Dupuis), who "came here with *David Copperfield in Taipei* ten years ago. Now she has an escort service." Besides Red Fish, the bad boys include Little Buddha; Hong Kong, a babe-magnet whom the others use to lure women to their flat; and Luen, a recent enrollee in the Fagin-like Red Fish's crime school. Luen acts as translator and seems to have a heart.

Jay, the ringmaster/Greek chorus for all this nightlife, and a rather conventional device for Yang, introduces this array of misfits, placing Marthe (or Marta, as she is dubbed by the boys, after the company that runs the city's subway system) on the outskirts of the moral neighbor-hood. She is a true innocent, or so we are led to believe, who actually thinks she will win Markus back with her unannounced visit—but who, of course, was naive enough to believe in him in the first place. Ginger, sensing an untapped resource, tries to recruit Marta for her talent pool almost immediately upon her arrival at the club, witnessing the discomfiture Marta's arrival has caused both Markus and Allison (who screams blue murder) and knowing that the poor girl is going to be in need of a friend.

Red Fish, seeing the non-Mandarin-speaking Marta getting ripped off by a taxi driver, comes to her rescue, and he even spots her three nights in a hotel. But his magnanimity is hardly without calculation.

"She'll be useful to us," he tells Luen. "Wait and see." Yang's Taipei runs on money and self-interest, the latter knowing no bounds.

Mahjong is a jarring construct, a little like Red Fish's assault on that pink Mercedes. Yang consistently uses the expectations we have about comedy, as well as some very broad assaults to the funny bone, to keep us off balance. The amount of human exploitation—or, rather, the casual manner in which humans are exploited or set up to be—in the film gives *Mahjong* an underlying tone of desperate sadness, despite the slapstick and baggy-pants sensibility. The way Yang presents it all, by making brutal violence a counterpoint to laughs, or by making ignorance or guile a part of what initially seems like an attempt at humor, renders *Mahjong* a far more disturbing film than its mere storyline or actions would suggest on their own.

Consider, for instance, the scene with Allison, who has wound up spending the night with Hong Kong after her contretemps with Markus at the club. Hong Kong, Red Fish, Buddha, and Luen all share the apartment, and—as they try to convince Allison—they share each other's girlfriends, too. They are a strange pack of monsters: they consider kissing bad luck ("Why kiss when you can fuck?" Buddha wants to know). Although they know it is a delicate operation they have undertaken, they don't really seem to know what is wrong with coercing Allison into a casual ménage à cinq.

The scene in which they team up on her, verbally at this point, is shot through a bedroom doorway, a signature Yang-ism. Doorways often provide a zone of transition and calamity and a perspective that gives the scene additional gravity if taken in light of Yang's work in general. The more insidious scene, however, is between Allison and Red Fish, who takes her aside to an adjoining bedroom, ostensibly to protect her. But there he proceeds to convince her that the four men's friendship depends on sharing—that if she does what they want, she will be showing how much she loves Hong Kong, and how could he fail to love her back? After all she has done? That Allison goes along with this is indicative of a more-than-pliant mind. But it certainly illuminates Red Fish's talent for manipulation and his allegiance to his father's code of business: nobody knows what they want; people want to be told what to do.

Is this attitude far from Yang's personal point of view? Taken in the context of the filmmaker's other work, *Mahjong*, a strange, brave, and relatively small movie, makes many of the same points as *A Brighter Summer Day* or *Taipei Story*. People constantly act against their better nature, either because the world is skewed against them or because they truly think they are doing right. If this recalls the famous and oft-abused line from Renoir's *Rules of the Game* ("Everybody has their reasons"), it may just be accidental. Everyone, after all, *does* have his reasons. But Yang, like Renoir, believes in the essential humanity of people. Even the most loathsome of his characters, even the hardest, can be brought to their knees (literally, at least, in *Mahjong*) by finding themselves face-to-face with themselves.

In Hitchcock, it has been said, almost everyone is innocent; in Chabrol, everyone is guilty. In Yang, everyone is good, even if the best intentions can be rationalizations. Likewise, the most callow heart can take the noblest turn.

Take Winston Chen, Red Fish's elusive father, who serves in *Mahjong* as that particularly Yangian character who despite his small screen time possesses enormous moral impact. His absence for most of *Mahjong* mirrors the absence—or impotence, or passive hostility—of fathers throughout Yang's movies. While the director's relationship with his own father seems to have been solid, the Taiwanese "circumstance," that is, the national reliance on a sole leader or icon, Chiang Kai-shek, is reflected in Yang's use of the patriarch as fraud. In *Taipei Story*, the father is just wrong; in *Brighter Summer Day,* he betrays himself. In *That Day, on the Beach*, he makes a wasteland of his own children's lives.

But Winston Chen is actually a decent sort. Taken for a ride some ten years earlier by his former mistress, Angela, he recovered his financial footing in only one year, clearly through illegal means but proving himself regardless. His son idolizes him, which makes it all the tougher on him when Winston disappears.

In a scene with Red Fish's mother, who is torn between anxiety over money and anxiety over whether Winston is shacked up with one of his serial bimbos, the son berates her for her lack of insight. "You sleep with him for twenty years and you still don't understand him," he says. When he does find his father, he berates him for running scared, for not being home, for having other woman. "You're the most shameless crook in this shameless country," he tells Winston. But Winston has had an epiphany. "When you have money you find you want things that money can't buy," he tells his son, in a way that suggests he knows it is too late for Red Fish and that what Red Fish has become is the fault of his father. Winston has found new values, new virtues, through a young schoolteacher, whom Red Fish treats with complete contempt when they meet but who, to her credit, maintains her composure, trying only to do what is right for Winston. That the son finds them dead as the result of a suicide pact is the beginning of the end of Red Fish, who has to confront not just his true face, but the fact that his worldview, the one he inherited from Dad, has been abandoned by the same man on whom he has modeled his life.

It is this outrage, a rather transparent but no less effective vehicle for Yang's own outrage, that leads Red Fish to kill Mr. Chiu, the presumptive "sugar daddy" of the concubine Angela. Red Fish has wanted to take revenge on Angela, since it was she, after all, who ripped off his father ten years ago, sending Red Fish's parents into a financial tailspin. The confrontation between Red Fish and Chiu is a psychodrama of Taiwanese proportions. Don't kill me, I have a son, Chiu pleads, after having already been pumped full of lead by an overstimulated Red Fish. Let me see my son one last time, he pleads again, at which point Red Fish starts to lose it. "Why did you make us live filthy lives like yours?" he screams, acting in proxy for Chiu's own son. But it is not until Chiu tells him that Angela—the Angela whom Red Fish has gone to such lengths to disgrace—is not the Angela he wants, that it was a different Angela after all, that Red Fish suffers his final meltdown.

But before we get to that we have to crosscut to Luen and Marta. Luen, the sensitive member of Red Fish's crew, lives in a house full of transients to whom his father rents rooms; the strong suggestion is that, should someone want to rent it, Luen would have to vacate his own room. Meanwhile, however, he is juggling his love for Marta, his supposed allegiance to Red Fish, and Red Fish's plan to more or less sell Marta to Ginger and her escort service.

What gives? Sent to fetch Marta for a meeting with Red Fish and Ginger, Luen has to spill the real story. It's a prostitution ring and they want you, he tells Marta. When she decides to go, having weighed her lack of options, Luen is bereft. But Marta comes back, and Luen takes

Tang Congsheng (standing) and Gu Baoming, in
Mahjong.

her to his father's house, hiding her in a backstairs area where she can
sleep off her ills.

What is it she is sleeping off? Nervous exhaustion, most likely. In
any event, the scene between the drowsy Marta and the vigilant Luen
moves the film into a zone of tenderness it has not known before, and
which proves the malleability of Yang's cinema. It can go anywhere,
essentially, because he knows how to move it.

Against a background of songs like "Aquarius" and other American
infiltrations, we get several strictly comic scenes. One features Hong
Kong and Allison, the former almost disinterested in his girlfriend's anxieties, the latter smothering Hong Kong with needy pleading. "I'll have a
breakdown if you go," she virtually screams at him. "How did you cope
in the past?" he asks her, wondering if this is her standard M.O. or directed only at him. When he refers quite casually to Allison's night with
him—and Red Fish, Little Buddha, and Luen—she screams her outrage;
Yang's shots of the unimpressed Hong Kong are cruelly hilarious.

Hong Kong gets his comeuppance, though. Waiting for Angela at
her apartment, he is greeted first by Angela's pals, Winnie and Sylvia,
who arrive to have their way with him. Treating him in an even more

contemptible fashion than the boys had treated Allison, they reduce him to hysterical tears. It is a rather shattering, if not unwelcome, moment, Hong Kong crawling on the carpet, howling his outrage over his own humiliation and, you hope, the humiliation he has visited on others.

Even Yang can't take it, apparently. The camera drifts outside, giving us another glorious shot of the Taipei skyline, although Hong Kong can still be heard inside, howling.

Drifting across the night and stars, the shot settles on a rooftop hideout where Marta and Luen are tied up; like so many moments in *Mahjong,* it is a complete shift in tone, this time into gangster comedy. Held hostage by the two thugs who have been looking for Red Fish, Luen and Marta are waiting for the ransom—which isn't coming. "What should we do?" she asks him. What can they do? The thug on duty gets a call from his confederate, telling him that, yes, they indeed do have the wrong two and that he has to kill them. But Marta gets the drop on him—How? Who knows! This is comedy—and they deliver their former captor to Red Fish, who proceeds to beat him like a dog.

Marta's abandonment of Luen leads him to a crying jag that is really

Ke Yuluen (left), Wang Bosen (center), and Tang Congsheng, in *Mahjong.*

unsettling—he is clearly hysterical but the moment has a theatricality that suggests Yang is still yanking our chain. Then, in a blackout, Luen's crying is overwhelmed by someone laughing. It is Markus, in a car, ferrying Marta to some unknown destination. He's laughing about the boys calling her Marta. Then he starts talking about the subway company. "You know why they're so well known?" he asks. It's because they're so good at telling "these people" what they want. The city paid four times the going rate for a mass transit system that doesn't work, he says. "When you take the Confucius and Mao and Chiang Kai-shek out of their textbooks, they don't know who to believe, except to work harder and make more money."

And they have got plenty. I was so lucky to come here, Markus says, and he isn't going to tell anyone he knows about it: Taipei is going to be the center of the universe.

Markus will have to enjoy it without Marta, however. When he stops at a food stall, she slips out of the car and, in a scene worthy of Nora Ephron, Luen finds her in the street; they kiss. Fade to black and roll the credits. But against those credits, you don't hear music; you hear the noise of the crowded street. Yang might give us a fairy-tale ending but there's no happily-ever-after. The sound of the city is a haunting one, a music that heralds a new world not of love, necessarily, unless it is a love of self.

In *Mahjong*, Yang is devastating, in his quiet way, expressing a hopelessness, even an exasperation, about love and connections. This may be why he decides to give us a break with the movie's fairy-tale ending. Considering the overall attitude of *Mahjong*, however, any hint of Cinderella is as evanescent as a sigh.

Yi Yi

Yang might have called it *One Wedding and a Funeral*, if he had really wanted to make money. Variety reported that *Yi Yi (A One and a Two . . . ,* 2000) was 247th among the "top-grossing pics" of 2001, having made less than one-fortieth the domestic box office of *Harry Potter and the Sorcerer's Stone;* it did better than *Lumumba*, worse than *Panic*.

The film did win the Best Foreign Language Film award from the New York Film Critics Circle and was named Best Film of the Year by the National (U.S.) Society of Film Critics. It made top-ten lists every-where and, in the kind of moment that inspires cognitive dissonance, was reviewed on network television by one of America's premier critics, John Leonard, on *CBS Sunday Morning*. Predictably, it was ignored by the Academy Awards, for which *Crouching Tiger, Hidden Dragon* was both the Taiwanese Oscar nominee and Best Foreign Film.

None of this has much to do, perhaps, with the indisputable fact that *Yi Yi*—which in English means "a one and a two . . . ," implying a musical count as well as the multiple parallelisms that gallop through the movie—was the best film released in the United States during 2000/2001. That isn't saying much, or nearly enough, considering that the same period saw *American Pie 2, Dr. Doolittle 2,* and *Scary Movie 2.* You certainly couldn't have a *Yi Yi 2.* Nor could one imagine that *Yi Yi* had anything in common with a studio picture.

Three hours long, with no explosions and a murder that occurs off screen, *Yi Yi* stars actors who were largely amateurs (most remarkably, Jonathan Chang and Kelly Lee, who play brother and sister Yang-Yang and Ting-Ting). Yang has stated that the acting pool in Taiwan is so shal-low he would rather work with nonactors, and he has done it before. But while he wrangled wonderful performances out of his youngest cast members, you realize that they were merely as wonderful as they needed to be. The script doesn't call for much in the way of versatility or even interpretation, not from the kids at least. In retrospect, the film seems crafted that way. Chang is required to be cute, and is; Lee, when not being viewed in long shot, is required to be thoughtful.

The real performance comes from the veteran actor Wu Nianzhen, as NJ, the besieged and beset father of Yang-Yang and Ting-Ting. NJ's computer business is foundering, his wife runs off to a monastery when her mother has a disabling stroke, and, over the course of the film, he is presented with the dubious opportunity to relive the pivotal moment of his romantic life.

Wu is one of Taiwan's most prominent screenwriters, having begun in the 1980s to collaborate with his island's most renowned directors, including Yang on *That Day, on the Beach,* Hou Hsiao-hsien on *Dust in the Wind,* and Ann Hui on *Song of the Exile.* He is also a director himself, of *Buddha Bless America* in 1996 and, in 1994, *A Borrowed Life,* a film with a very Yang-like theme.

Wu's characterization of NJ might best be described as mournfully optimistic. And why not? NJ is, if nothing else, decent. He loves his children. He doesn't begrudge his wife her hysteria when she runs off with the monks. For a long time, he even humors his partners—whose firm needs an infusion of cash and ideas—especially when they act like idiots. The sensitive man destined to be damaged, he shows nothing but patience, and even a particular brand of restrained affection, toward his brother-in-law, A-Di, who owes NJ a lot of money and displays very little urgency about paying it back.

It is A-Di's wedding that opens the picture (a funeral closes it), and the joy could safely be called restrained. To the vaguely Celtic strain of fiddles and the sound of children's voices, *Yi Yi* begins with preparations for the wedding, which is an event, we are led to believe, desired by no one in particular, other than the very pregnant bride, Xiao Yan (played by Xiao Shushen). "We had bus rides without tickets in my day, too," one woman clucks. But A-Di's old girlfriend is taking it badly. "Where is that pregnant bitch?" howls Yun-Yun (Zeng Xinyi), having broken down in front of A-Di's Grandma (Tang Ruyun) and apologized for letting her grandson slip out of her grasp. Grandma is not happy about Xiao Yan; her disapproval is silent but very, very pointed. She would have preferred Yun-Yun. A-Di might have, too.

The atmosphere of domestic friction is in sharp contrast to the air surrounding NJ himself. He is always the deadpan, Keatonesque calm at the center of whatever storm is brewing or blowing. Distanced from, if not necessarily disapproving of, the drinking games played by A-Di's buddies, he reveals every now and then that the stress is getting to him. Like his friend Da Da (Michael Tao), who suddenly can't remember why he came down in an elevator, NJ is a quietly desperate man—a calmly coiled spring. When that same elevator opens and Sherry (Ke Suyun) walks out, NJ greets his long-lost girlfriend with something very close to physical paralysis. It is as if a prayer had been answered but he hadn't known he'd prayed.

Recrimination is a spark upon which *Yi Yi* lights many fires. "Why didn't you come that day?" Sherry cries to NJ, after their initial formalities. "I waited and waited. I never got over it." Neither did NJ, although Sherry's recriminations about that day seem to be much about loss of face; NJ's, directed at himself, are about a loss of years and a life he thinks imperfect.

Is it? He has nearly ideal children—beautiful, sensitive, generous, and unspoiled. Yang-Yang (we'll explain the names in a minute) is the artist-in-the-bud; Ting-Ting, less talented or attractive than, say, her cello-playing neighbor, Lili (Adrian Lin), is nevertheless an easily tortured soul, much like Dad, with whom she shares both a temperament and a fate. She is also inclined to brood, and the script gives her plenty to brood about.

Home from the wedding rehearsal and readying to leave again, NJ asks Ting-Ting to be sure to take out the garbage. She takes out some but not all of it, her attention diverted by a couple she sees below her window. They inspire a kind of reverie in Ting-Ting, who clearly idealizes the pair she sees—her neighbor Lili and Lili's boyfriend, Fatty—as the embodiment of romantic passion. In doing so, Ting-Ting crystallizes one of the film's recurring themes, how we impose the personal on any given picture. As we'll learn later, there is nothing ideal about Lili and Fatty.

Ting-Ting forgets the garbage bag and later, after Grandma has the stroke that summons the family home, will be told the old woman was found collapsed by the dustbins (consigned there, it seems, like a bit of history). No one figures out what happened, and Ting-Ting never tells. But the circumstances gnaw at her throughout the picture.

When Yang, especially early in his career, was compared to Michelangelo Antonioni, it was for his meditative gaze, cool detachment, sense of modern malaise, and philosophical awareness of the ambiguity of the image. But if Antonioni is Beckett, Yang is Joyce—at least by the time of *Yi Yi*, which is a Taiwanese *Ulysses* in its all-encompassing context, as well as its characterizations.

If you pursue this bit of literary gamesmanship, Ting-Ting is Bloom (so is NJ) and Yang-Yang is Stephen Dedalus. In the very first scene, set apart by his sober black tuxedo (the other little boys wear the more ostentatious white), Yang-Yang is teased relentlessly by the girls at the wedding. They pursue him later at school and everywhere he goes. He is too cute to leave alone, but that's not what he knows. All he knows is that they are making him miserable, and he can't see them coming. He wants eyes in the back of his head. He wants to see what others can't. He also wants to know what others don't. And he wants to tell them all about it.

Yang-Yang's dilemma is a simple but eloquent allegory for the birth of the artist, and art. Aptly enough, Yang-Yang—can his name designate him as anything other than a stand-in for the director?—also exists within a universe (or at least a storyline) parallel to the rest of the movie. While Ting-Ting's and NJ's stories run beside each other like train tracks, their destinations all but preordained, Yang-Yang rides some unguided missile toward artistic epiphany. He gets a camera, and he takes pictures of mosquitoes, which no one can see; later, he shoots the backs of people's heads. "You can't see it yourself," he tells A-Di, "so I help you."

Yang-Yang has his inaugural moment of artistic lucidity in one of those scenes Yang habitually includes in his films, of the type that completely transcends the action and certainly loosens any literary tethers that might attach his film to the ground, releasing it—no, propelling it—into a visual ether. Having bombed one of his tormenters, the school disciplinarian, with water balloons, Yang-Yang flees to a schoolroom where a nature film is being shown. As he settles in, the Tall Girl arrives. The pet of that same teacher, the Strict Disciplinarian, this girl has been one of Yang-Yang's abusers, too, but she has also inspired his awe. Watching her in the swimming pool will inspire the boy to practice breathing under water in the bathroom sink and eventually prompt him to jump in over his head (an apt but soggy metaphor for love).

During the classroom movie, the girl walks in and is captured in the projector's stream. Clouds are racing by; she's sanctified by light and sex. "That was the beginning of everything," the film's narrator says. It certainly is for Yang-Yang.

Yang the director exists in Yang-Yang the child, but he also exists in NJ. ("You pushed me to become an engineer," NJ says to Sherry, during their liaison in Japan; Yang himself was educated as an engineer in the United States and worked in the field for years before moving on to film.) Like the Man in the Brown Macintosh who pops in and out of *Ulysses* (and is, indeed, a stand-in for the author of that book), Ota, the Japanese computer genius whom NJ is dispatched to recruit, is Yang himself, visiting his film.

With his crewneck sweaters and vaguely Moe Howard hair, Ota

looks a bit like Bill Gates (which Yang said was inadvertent), but the hair evokes Yang, too—as does the fact that Ota is a director, of whatever context in which he finds himself. At their first meeting, NJ watches as Ota gets a pigeon to sit on his shoulder. It is our tipoff: people might lie, but not nature. Ota is on the level. Oddly forthright, candid, unlike any of the people NJ knows in business in Taipei, Ota gets an immediate and positive response from NJ. They speak English, their only common language. "You are like me," Ota says. "We can't tell a lie."

NJ has been sent by his partners to deal with Ota, because he looks honest. How ironic, Yang wants us to know, that he actually is.

Later, Ota will meet with both NJ and Sherry, while the two are having their reunion in Tokyo. Ota knows all, even if he occasionally feints. "You are his music," Ota says to Sherry, having been told by NJ that she never liked music because there was "no profit in it." (Consider Yang's fascination with music; that his wife, the pianist Peng Kaili, performs on the film's soundtrack; that Ota himself performs, beautifully, the Japanese pop hit "Sukiyaki," or "Ue O Muite Aruko," in the piano bar he visits with NJ. Do we need to know any more about Sherry?)

During their final meeting, even as NJ's partners are pulling the rug out from under their deal back in Taipei, Ota shows NJ a card trick. He knows where each card is in the deck. And it's no trick. "I trained myself to know where each one is," he says. He also knows the deal is dead. When NJ looks to tell him so in the morning, Ota, like the pigeons, has already flown the coop.

Ota knows all, of course, not because it is a trick, but because it is his movie. "You are young people," he tells NJ and Sherry, a statement that can be considered only if you know the entire story, that as a couple they are in the act of reliving their youth. In a parallel universe—embodied by Fatty and Ting-Ting—it is also being relived for them.

Up to a point, what we see in Fatty and Lili is a typically tormented teenage romance: angry storm-offs, notes being furtively passed. Lili's home life is disturbed, profoundly and irreparably, but we don't know as yet to what degree. Her mother, Mrs. Jiang (Xu Shuyuan), brings home various men, to Lili's evident distaste. Loud and angry fights, between Mom and those men, or Lili and Mom, break out within earshot of Ting-Ting's apartment. Mrs. Jiang appears in the morning in sunglasses, apparently meant to hide a shiner. Fatty, who at first wants Ting-Ting to pass notes on to Lili—which she initially refuses to do—starts giving Ting-Ting notes of her own.

It is through Ting-Ting that we get the malleability of perception and of conscience. She berates Fatty for abusing Lili but is in fact drawn to him herself; we see them, in a restaurant, via one of Yang's favorite devices, glass that both reflects and distorts. Ting-Ting's moral quandary is written on the window of the restaurant, where she's sitting with Fatty. She has berated the boy for being unkind to Lili. But in Ting-Ting's innocent mind, she has just betrayed Lili herself.

Of course, Ting-Ting thinks she knows what's going on. She doesn't. Stepping off an elevator, she finds herself in an eye-lock with Lili, who is standing in the doorway of her apartment, stock still, staring and uttering a miserable "How can this be?!!" Ting-Ting thinks—we can see it on her face—that Lili is upset with her. But what is happening is much more serious: Lili has discovered her mother in bed with her English teacher (who, we will learn later, has been sleeping with Lili, too). While all hell breaks loose, Ting-Ting has an epiphany of her own, not of art but of adulthood. The egocentrism of childhood vanishes in that instant when she realizes that life has gone on around her in ways she could never have suspected, bursting the bubble of her adolescent insularity.

Ting-Ting's breakthrough helps her in the way she copes with her ailing grandmother. In the beginning, when the family was instructed to keep moving Grandma to prevent bedsores, and to pat her back to maintain circulation, they were also told they had to talk to her, to mitigate the effects of the stroke on her mind (even though the woman really does seem gone for good). Ting-Ting does these things, guiltily touching the old woman's hand and having a reunion with her in a dream. Yang-Yang cannot talk to Grandma at all, although he will tell her why during the moving words he speaks to her at her funeral at the end of movie. But Ting-Ting's gift is the realization that what happened to Grandma—and what happened to Ting-Ting herself, to NJ, and to everyone around her—largely happened beyond her control.

Yi Yi is unquestionably Yang's crowning achievement thus far in a career with miles to go. It is a movie of multiple characters (and personalities) and multiple formal themes and devices:

Doorways/Thresholds. Doorways are sanctuaries, providing—even though the characters seldom realize it—a point of return before the step into some new phase, some new dilemma. They grant a kind of magical moment of indecision. Or un-decision. Or limbo. Yang's penchant for this kind of framing is evident in every one of his films, but it reaches the proportions of a fetish in *Yi Yi,* and on a kind of graduated scale. When Yang-Yang stands within a door frame before snapping his first photographs, and thus ritualistically inaugurates his life as an artist, it is an important, albeit benign, moment. When caught on the cusp of deciding how she will or will not lead her moral life, and whether she will relive her father's, Ting-Ting stands under a railroad trestle, a doorway of almost comically exaggerated proportions.

Reflections and Truth. The ambiguity of the visual image mirrored—flopped, as a photo editor would say; lying, as Susan Sontag might have said—is a recurring visual theme in *Yi Yi,* one that suggests a moral uncertainty. The manner in which characters are reflected—in restaurant windows, car windshields, and, of course, each other's eyes—is all about the myriad interpretations that we can impose on what we see. In *Yi Yi* much of the storyline trips along on misapprehension and overly egocentric points of view (see Ting-Ting). Like Yang-Yang, Yang is helping us out.

A-Di. NJ's brother-in-law is a category unto himself—a pig, essentially, and a moral reprobate who is the opposite of NJ or for that matter Ota, NJ's soul brother. He is a deadbeat, a hustler, an adulterer; he is superstitious to such a degree that his baby is left unnamed at the end of the film because he can't decide on a name lucky enough to counter the child's bad-luck birthday. He certainly has no talent for introspection, and when introspection is forced on him—after his wife and girlfriend kick off a near-slapstick melee at a party of friends—he proves himself a coward, opting for suicide, although he can't (or claims not to) remember the details later.

A-Di, obese in body and appetites, does talk to Grandma, or rather, lies to her: "People come to me for loans," he tells her, although he has yet to repay his debt to NJ. The $9 million Yun-Yun loaned him to pay NJ back? He gave it to someone named Piggy to invest—and Piggy has left the country. Turned out of his own house by his bride, A-Di ends up temporarily with Yun-Yun, in her bed, watching porn.

Although *Yi Yi* largely is about family—and love, and our utter solitude—A-Di is a flashback to Yang's Taipei-as-capital-of-global-avarice films, particularly *Mahjong*, into which A-Di would have fit naturally, because of his singular self-interest and megalomaniacal perspective. (As if to make that very point, Yang has Ting-Ting hear a news report about Marta, the Taiwanese transportation company that figured in *Mahjong* and in the nicknaming of the character in that film played by Virginie Ledoyen.)

Americanisms. NJ takes an unhappy Yang-Yang to McDonald's during the wedding rehearsal, thus making his son visibly happy. Hey, why not, it's a Happy Meal. Artists have to eat, too. Ting-Ting, Lili, and Fatty make a couple of trips to a place called NY Bagels, where someone always seems to get into an argument. The locales, amusingly incongruous to Western eyes, personify imported consumerism in its most literal representation.

Names. Yang-Yang is just the most obvious of several name games played in *Yi Yi*. Min-Min, Ting-Ting, Yun-Yun, even Lili, are all singsong couplings that imply the double lives their owners lead. (Ota is the ethical computer genius; Ato is the owner of the copycat company with whom NJ's partners sign.) Another game is the juxtaposition of similar names, such as those of the neighboring families, the Jians and the Jiangs; one is a relatively stable nuclear unit, but the other is headed by a single mother who, with her daughter, ends up in the middle of a crime of passion.

Religion, or Is It Just Superstition? Min-Min, NJ's wife, runs off with the monks after her mother has a stroke—on the luckiest day of the year, according to A-Di. Her religious retreat isn't about moral sustenance but about finding an escape from her problems. But that is the point you get, via Yang. When Min-Min brings the monks home to meet NJ, he is confused about their motives, saying he intends to stay where he is, that he has never had a problem with which he needed to ask God's help. "A purified soul makes it easier for God to answer prayers," he is told. NJ, having suddenly received the gift of enlightenment, asks, "Do you take checks?"

Yang seems as suspicious, even contemptuous, of organized religion as he is of middle-aged women. There is very little conventional spirituality in his films. When spiritual representations do appear, they arrive via S'ir's holy-roller sister in *A Brighter Summer Day* or the moneygrubbing monks of *Yi Yi,* embodiments of a worldview that suggests that organized religion has served the cause of oppression over the course of humankind's history and is an opiate the masses don't need. At the comatose Grandma's bedside, NJ compares talking to her to prayer. "I'm not sure," he says, "the other party can hear me."

The Ineluctable Importance of the Insignificant. A bag of garbage starts the whole ball rolling.

Motherhood. We haven't dealt with Min-Min, the mother of Ting-Ting and Yang-Yang, played by Elaine Jin (who starred in Yang's *That Day, on the Beach*). In many ways, she is far more important to the point of *Yi Yi* than her lack of screen time would seem to indicate.

In the beginning of the film, she could be described by extremely charitable people as self-absorbed—by others, perhaps, as a bitch on wheels. Reminiscent of the mother in *A Brighter Summer Day,* who hopes she won't have to buy her son eyeglasses because they are too expensive, she exudes coldness, a general sourness, toward her husband and her children. Although it is Min-Min's mother—hers and A-Di's—who has the stroke, the older woman is left in her son-in-law NJ's care. Min-Min fills a particular role that is consistent in the films of Edward Yang, that of the less-than-maternal mother. Where Min-Min differs from her predecessors, however, is that she actually, physically, leaves, while the father—the usual absentee in Yang's films—never really does.

It is Grandma, comatose yet somehow the locus of all concerns, who causes Min-Min's crisis. "I haven't anything to say to Mother," Min-Min cries to NJ. "I live a blank." Although she can say this about her life, it is clearly meant to be about her, not NJ or her kids or her mother or any spiritual void she imagines herself to be feeling. She leaves the house, and the movie, essentially, returning only near the end, when she goes into hysterics beside her mother's casket.

"How can you leave us!!!" she wails. "How can A-Di and I go on without you." It is a mercifully brief scene; unless you are paying extremely close attention you might not even notice that it is Min-Min having the breakdown at all. But it is. And her grief is something awful. Why? When NJ enters the room, he sits not with his wife but with Ting-Ting, who for all intents and purposes is his spiritual doppelganger. Ting-Ting has traversed the same emotional territory as NJ over the previous few days and has helped put his regrets in order. Min-Min, on the other hand, is at the gateway to a new frontier, one of self-justification, self-recrimination, contrition, and remorse, for having abandoned her mother at her moment of death, and for God knows what crimes over the course of her life.

Min-Min is all alone. Yang-Yang is all alone, too, in his special way, and his life will be particularly burdened precisely because he is special. But unlike Yang-Yang, Min-Min is alone without a point or an aim.

Despite the movie's warmth and generosity, solitude is a key to *Yi Yi*. Everyone in *Yi Yi* is alone, because as Yang-Yang says, they can't see it all. We don't live others' lives; we can't read their souls, and because we can't we will always exist in our own little worlds. Ting-Ting misinterprets what is going on with Lili and Fatty. Sherry never really knew NJ, only the kind of life she wanted to live and the man she thought could provide it. For most of the movie, NJ doesn't really know himself or what he wants. By the end he is more or less reconciled, but he still doesn't know his wife or Sherry, and Yang-Yang, whom he loves, promises to befuddle him for life. NJ knows Ting-Ting, and much better than he even suspects, because they have shared the same experience. But again, they can't know that and never will.

It is left to someone like Yang-Yang, or Yang himself, to fill in the gaps, to provide the common language—the artistic mortar—that will conjoin this great cracked mosaic of humanity. The reason *Yi Yi* is such an emotional experience for so many people is that, in it, the director acknowledges the unspoken, even unconscious, desire among people everywhere to escape the abstract loneliness that life has forced upon them. Which is why people cry at *Yi Yi* and probably always will.

An Interview with Edward Yang |

The following was consolidated from interviews I conducted at the 2000 Cannes Film Festival, where *Yi Yi* was in competition and Yang won Best Director; the 2001 Cannes Film Festival, at which Yang served on the jury; and via e-mails exchanged during late 2001 and early 2002.

JOHN ANDERSON: What is it that makes being a Taiwanese filmmaker unique?

EDWARD YANG: One of the unique things about doing films in Taiwan in general is [that] because [of] the past political leadership—it's very much like China—they don't want to do very constructive things with cultural matters, or anything that improves people's intelligence. Really. Honestly. They have certain rules you follow, and they encourage everyone to go into science, engineering, mathematics, anything practical, so the college entrance exams—in humanities, they give low scores to discourage you, mark you down. They try to convince parents to create a social value that says these are the less important people in the society, so that people talented in these fields have to be very interested in this work.

One of my classmates is now the leading sociologist in Taiwan and when he decided to go into sociology and take the entrance exam for university, he was a very, very good student and his father was a very well-educated scholar, and he decided to go into sociology very, very early and all the teachers tried to discourage him. "This is not good for you," they said, put him under all sorts of pressure.

I was practically the same way, but I gave in. I'd wanted to go into architecture, because I thought that was the only field that balanced humanity and technology, but I didn't get in, so I went into engineering. But the media in Taiwan reflects this attitude. People in the arts are not much better than some whore down the street.

JA: You have an example?

EY: Sure. The other day, we had a party screening; the little boy who's in *Yi Yi* was there and this other movie star came from Hong Kong, Shu Qi, who's in another film here, she came in with all her entourage, and the journalists, the photographers, they kept after her to bend over the little boy so that her breasts were hanging out of her dress. The next day my wife called me from home and said, "It's really bad; the picture's all over the papers in Taiwan." That's terrible. It's tabloid stuff. But the attitude, it's like she did it on purpose.

It's such a very bad image that's been created that not that many people are interested in this field, especially acting. Some, of course, are very interested and there are very good actors, but not such a big pool. Every time I have a story, there aren't enough quality actors to choose from, so I've gotten very, very used to working with nonactors—not just children, but older people, too. Even the guy who plays the father, he's a great actor but no one wanted to use him in a leading role. This is the first time, and I knew he would do the best job.

JA: So conditions in the Taiwan film industry are rather dire?

EY: Basically, commercial cinema disappeared earlier than art-house. When we started working, when the New Wave started, there was a very welcoming thing for the audiences. All the films actually sold more tickets. The Taiwanese supported it; it was a refreshing thing.

Also, I think it's not really not commercial. The films just targeted a certain group of consumers in the city who were better educated and in a lot of ways offered them more interesting subject matter.

JA: What were conditions when you started?

EY: The Central Motion Picture Corporation party studio used to own everything. And the guy at the head of it, he was cheated for so many projects. He spent millions and millions of dollars to make some policy films no one was going to go to, and I remember also, he was so pissed at one guy for spending $100,000 on coffee. He was really mad. So this top guy decided to give the young guys a break, with a very small budget of about $150,000—which is a lot of coffee—and that film was made by four different directors, four episodes that sort of moved from private school to high school to college and into society.

People loved it. They gave it a six-day run, and it made money—another $150,000 on top of its budget, so everyone else got a project, and that was my first feature.

JA: And everything, of course, went smoothly?

EY: At the beginning no one would even work for us. "We've been here for twenty years and these guys think they're directors!" My first day, I had drawn everything, storyboarded everything, but the cameraman was so terrible; every shot was a struggle. "An experienced director can do thirty-five shots a day," he said. "See how many you can do." At the end of the day I was on my thirty-third shot. Then the guy said, "No, I'm not going to do this one." I said, "What do you mean?" I was ready to beat the guy up.

The next day I got the other three directors together and said, "We have to stick together on this; if I get kicked out because of this, you guys are going to lose this project." But as we went on, things improved. And, of course, we were all glad the public responded.

JA: Has *Yi Yi* been a gratifying experience?

EY: Oh, yeah. Absolutely.

JA: You spoke a lot about the culture of Taiwan, how the culture was skewed toward getting kids to pursue sciences rather than arts. You had to go outside Taiwan to finance *Yi Yi?*

EY: Yes, it was Japanese money, venture capital money.

JA: So what was the reaction in Taiwan to *Yi Yi?*

EY: It hasn't been released yet [as of May 2001]. It's a pretty depress-

Edward Yang (center), with Jonathan Chang (left) and Kelly Lee on the red carpet before the official screening of *Yi Yi* at the Cannes Film Festival, 2000.

ing situation, to say the least. Local films only amount to a tiny percentage of the market. I think it has a lot to do with how these distributors work. In my view, I'm more and more certain that they're simply not good business people. And it's not how great the Hollywood products are; they're just easier to get into the theaters and the locals couldn't raise any competition. They'd get wiped out. So they look for protection from the government. It's easy money and they don't have to go out and build a business.

But I think the business of Asian film is changing, comparing [it] to last year and especially after the success of *Crouching Tiger* and my film and Wong Kar-wai's film [*In the Mood for Love*].

JA: Yours and Lee's films were successful outside Taiwan.

EY: Oh, yes, and that I think is a positive thing.

JA: Isn't it strange that Taiwanese directors are loved everywhere in the world except Taiwan?

EY: Actually, it says a lot about the culture, the way things are going, and also it has a lot to do with the media. Basically, they . . . I have a lot of trouble with, well, everything. Really. It's a total reverse of what democracy is supposed to be. And this year I'm much more angry than last year because of all these developments, in the arts as much as anything else. The unemployment rate is high. It's so funny; actually, so much of it is laughable. For instance, in Taiwan they say, "Oh, the Europeans, the socialist countries, they have an unemployment rate of 10, 11 percent, that's terrible." They laugh at the Europeans. So this year they say, "We have a 4 percent unemployment rate." It's higher than that, actually. But then a friend of mine told me, "This is bullshit. The 4 percent, it's not the employment population, it's the entire population. When the Europeans say 10, 11 percent they're talking about the employable population." What? It's at least three times that, 12 percent. Nothing to laugh at. It gets to you.

JA: You lived for how many years in the States?

EY: Eleven years all told.

JA: You ever think about going back, permanently?

EY: Well, right now, basically, I'm in Taipei only half the time. I have to be in Hong Kong, Tokyo, sometimes here, L.A. It varies.

JA: But your closest thing to a permanent home is still in Taipei?

EY: Basically. My wife's from there; my wife's family is taking care of the kid there right now.

JA: Are your parents alive?

EY: Yeah, they're in Seattle. What's funny is in the jury meeting here [at Cannes] someone will be thinking, "Oh, yes, he's American enough!" [laughs]. Someone else will be thinking I'm not American enough—maybe I like Joel Coen's movie or something.

JA: My understanding is you come from a pretty well-to-do family.

EY: Not really. Middle, right in the middle. My dad had to go to

Shanghai to work, because he was sending his paycheck back to the village, just about the whole amount. This is in the thirties, even the twenties. He left home when he was fifteen. My mom also traveled a lot because her father worked for American missionaries. He was in jail, because he worked for a warlord—he could read and write and the warlord he worked for lost everything to another warlord, so my grandfather was thrown in jail, just for working for the guy.

JA: This sounds like the feudal period?

EY: Absolutely. There was also this American priest who was helping prisoners and he found my grandfather could read and write, so he asked him to help as his assistant in the prison. Soon, he grew to like him, so he talked the warlord into letting my grandfather go. After that, my grandfather became a Christian; my mom was born into a Christian family. And my dad, to save money, stayed at the YMCA—so that's how my mom met my dad, sometime during the war. They were all away from their families, traveling. They were the first generation of middle-class, salary-class people and had to follow their employer, which happened to be the state-owned bank.

JA: Both of them?

EY: Both of them. Different branches. But they all moved to Taipei; I was born in Shanghai, where the banks were.

JA: Somebody told me, "Oh, yeah, Edward Yang, he comes from a very rich family, he can finance his own movies if he wants to."

EY: Every place is like last year's U.S. election. There are city folk, noncity folk, and this polarity is becoming more and more extreme and the antagonism also is just like the election: all the midwestern states voted for Bush, the coastal states voted for Gore.

Taiwan is the same way. I represent basically the urban intellectual and then there are the big powers that still remain in the not-so-educated, easily manipulated population. When the media is involved, especially when the media is not that independent, they side with the power and start to color things in a certain direction. There's a lot of that. When *A Brighter Summer Day* came out I was shocked to read some of the more radical people said, "This is a story to slander localism from someone who was not born in Taiwan."

JA: And they also use the fact that you lived eleven years in the United States?

EY: Oh, yes.

JA: You recognize a big American influence on your work, dating back to your youth?

EY: One of the things about that, and especially rock 'n' roll music, is that it reflects the time—for us, at that time, kids didn't believe in the government; they'd simply lost confidence in anything the government said. I think young kids can sense something at a very young age that I, at least, couldn't quite articulate. I didn't think much of Chiang Kai-shek; he wasn't anything great. When they wanted me to say he's great, I'd say, "He's great," but in my mind I'm saying, "Bullshit." I didn't want to spend one extra minute on him. But the thing that interested me and a lot of my friends were Japanese comics and American rock 'n' roll. Those things were new, every week. You know? Japanese comics, every week you had a new one, the story went on for another twenty pages. And for rock 'n' roll, the new *Billboard* charts came out, you had a new No. 1. That, to us, was more believable.

JA: And it was up-to-date?

EY: Oh, yeah. The reason why we loved it was very simple: because Taiwan was influenced strictly by Japan and the U.S. We had these channels to be exposed to other things, so why not? To us they were more believable, more trustworthy[,] and again gave us room to imagine things. I still feel very lucky to have lived through that period, where even though there was a propaganda machine, we didn't believe in it. Not like today. Today, if I were a kid, I would wind up spending twenty-four hours a day just reading through all the bullshit in the newspapers and television trying to tell me what to buy. I wouldn't have time to just sit and think.

JA: You mean you'd be so overwhelmed by marketing?

EY: Yeah. I think kids nowadays have less time to let things soak in. People think, "Oh, these kids all just go to McDonald's." I don't think it's a McDonald's problem. I think it's more like, "What happened to the free time we used to have?" We used to hang out. It was time to . . . at least we tried something to see if it worked, or didn't work, and we learned something. Nowadays, they're spoon fed and you don't learn anything. You end up just pulling money out of your pocket.

I think, especially for Asian kids, you learn from school that it's good to conform. But it's bad not to have time to think, "Hey, is that right or wrong?" They don't seem to have that nowadays. I'm glad we used to have time—time not to believe, even though we tried to pretend we had conformed.

JA: Were you also watching American movies at the same time when you were a kid?

EY: Oh, yes. Actually, I just recently, the last month, it just dawned on me why the Taiwanese New Wave had so much to do with my generation. My generation grew up watching all kinds of movies in the world. Fellini. Bresson. I wonder if I told you this last year, but I wouldn't have been thinking this way. This year it makes a lot of difference. We were brought up on a lot of movies.

JA: But did that then change?

EY: You know why? Because Taiwan at the time was supported by the United States, which recognized it as the only official government of China. So we tried to stay diplomatically attached to all the countries of the world. And one of the things the government did was import all their films.

JA: That makes sense.

EY: And the government also took over a lot of films from the Japanese and assigned them: "These two cinemas have to show Japanese films; these two show Italian films." So we get to see Italian films, French films, Spanish films, American films, British films, all the films in the world.

JA: And it was all current?

EY: Yeah, yeah, and every time they'd show a film they'd have to explain in the papers things like, "This guy is Ingmar Bergman. It's not Ingrid Bergman . . ." [laughs].

JA: Taipei must have been a great movie town.

EY: At the time, for us, we were exposed to everything. They'd go to second run, third run, and a lot of kids saw these films. But now I begin to think it must have a lot to do with what happened, because these things are in our memories. At the time, we didn't have television. It must have made a big difference.

JA: So, presumably, Taiwan's population has a great thirst for cinema. Why isn't it more successful?

EY: The last few years, I've tried to show people that this is a workable, profitable business.

JA: I know the United States is problematic, because it's becoming increasingly hard to get foreign movies in. Are there a huge number of Taiwanese films we don't get to see?

EY: No. Basically, the amount of production is so low. And now what's really fucked up is the subsidy program. All these distributors got together, it's a terrible thing. They have all these trade unions under their control, so they came in with the story that they represent the trade unions, and government bureaucrats want the trade unions to give up, so they basically run the subsidy program. Every time I make a statement, they'll have their media people, those journalists, write something nasty about me, how I'm criticizing the society, I don't love the country, I don't love Taiwan, I'm more of a Chinese mainlander. They want to paint a very ugly picture of me, because they think I'm a threat.

JA: People don't see through this kind of thing?

EY: Less and less. Less and less. A very few courageous people. But less and less. So I just do my own thing.

JA: There are very specific stylistic choices made in your movies, very specific influences. Was there a point at which you made an aesthetic decision about how you were going to make movies?

EY: I think it had to do not just with movies. A lot has to do with Japanese comics, American comics, and also painting. I started painting quite young. My dad, he would go to the movies but he also paints, watercolors, that's his pastime.

JA: And he did this when you were young?

EY: Yes, my brother and I, whatever he was doing, we would play with. Also, later, music. I loved music . . .

JA: You play music?

EY: No, but the love of music is also from my dad. He didn't really understand that much about music, but he had this friend who would tell him what to listen to. So he tried, but I don't think he ever totally understood all the music he listened to.

JA: Classical music?

EY: Everything. His friend was also a neighbor and lived behind us and I remember he used to collect—he wasn't a wealthy guy, he was also on salary—but his hobby was to listen to music. Basically, he'd just play with the record player. He was an audiophile.

JA: I've known plenty of people who know nothing about music but know everything about the equipment.

EY: Yeah, yeah, right. That was him. So we were listening to rock 'n' roll and my dad really frowned on it. He would play classical and thought that was supposed to be the thing we should be listening to.

JA: But it was Western music he was listening to?

EY: Mostly. Eastern music or Chinese music, there's very few pieces; even the pop music, you have very few songs. That's the Chinese culture—it's not like later on, when pop music became a business. Earlier on, there was very little work, you're not encouraged to do art. And also when my dad was growing up, those kinds of professions belonged to the, uh . . .

JA: Undesirables?

EY: Or prostitutes, basically. Actors were the lower rank of society. Until later on, when they realized, "Hey, in Western society this is considered a good thing." Then the level started to rise. Another thing, Taiwan's popular music—we never had our own popular music until the late seventies, early eighties, and it coincided with the New Wave cinema; it's really about the generational thing. My generation began to feel so confident that we were taking over. Even though there was still censorship when we started making films, there was censorship, but we didn't care. And also at the time there was a New Wave in music which was very, very influenced by rock 'n' roll and also the sixties antiwar songs—Bob Dylan, Joan Baez, and all them.

JA: So you were listening to that stuff?

EY: Well, the Taiwanese music was entirely influenced by that.

JA: And they didn't censor it?

EY: They couldn't do anything anymore. They wanted people to change their lyrics. They were asked to go into the Censorship Bureau and were told, "Hey, you need to change this lyric into this" and the guys would be like "Fuck you," they'd just turn over the desk. They couldn't do anything about it. So we got more and more confident that these guys couldn't do anything to us. The only thing they could do is get the record company not to release your album. But then, at the time, there was no money anyway. And the pirated version would sell for six, seven times the price of the legal ones.

So, for us, we were very open, especially my generation. 'Cause at the time the kids—my dad was quite rare—the kids were trying to find things on our own. We'd get together and someone would say, "Hey, this Japanese comic's *great*," and we'd all get on it, and that was fun . . .

JA: It was about discovering things.

EY: Yes, yes, and that's the kind of thing kids nowadays don't have. Things go to them. They don't have to explore things.

JA: Is it the same in Taiwan as in the United States? Years ago there were things that were considered indecent; there's very little now considered indecent. But wasn't the risqué quality of something the thing that sometimes got your interest as a kid?

EY: I think kids nowadays in Taiwan, especially since I was teaching—basically, I was fired, because I was too Left. And gradually I realized, from class to class, that they're more and more conservative.

JA: You were teaching film? At what level?

EY: The university level. I stopped in 1995. It was about film, or just creativity. I used film to say why this guy or that guy is so great. I tried to inspire the kids just to be more comfortable with themselves. So the first homework was for them to write something about the most memorable thing in their life. And through that process I could guide them to why is this so unforgettable, analyze the situations, inspire them to tell a story, see if the elements would make the story impressive. Things like that. Basically, it was a pretty open class. At the first gathering I was like, "If you don't want to listen to me, you don't have to show up. You'll get a grade." But I wanted everyone who was participating to interact, and so forth. So I was considered too radical. Also, the trend is more and more to the right.

JA: Isn't it also amazing what people aren't familiar with? I hear stories from teachers of film school students who show up and don't know what *Citizen Kane* is. You get that kind of thing?

EY: The problem with the school I was teaching in—the name of the school was the National Academy of Fine Arts. I was in the theater department. All the students were accepted not just by the written exam, but they needed to go through auditions and stuff. The audition process began . . . began to suck. And the teachers' mentality began to change. Less and less liberal to more and more conservative. More and more conventional. So one time, one of the kids who was in my movie, Zhang Zhen, had acted in films already—he was in *Crouching Tiger,* the fellow who plays the bandit who falls in love with Zhang Ziyi—*he* wasn't accepted, simply because they didn't want him. He *has* to be qualified; he's an experienced actor. So how can you turn down a qualified person like that?

JA: They turned him down on the basis of what?

EY: They probably thought that they couldn't control him, or impress him enough. But basically it was getting very conservative, conventional, and conformist. And I just got an amazing story today. I called my office and my assistant—we work together on the acting workshop and stuff—he said, "You know what? ASA computer headquarters was burned down." The fire raged on for two days, two full days, forty-some hours.

JA: In Taipei?

EY: In Taipei. And the loss was $5 billion. ASA computer was started by my classmates; they're all billionaires.

JA: They don't finance your films?

EY: Ha, no. But it just says so much about Taiwan. Now these guys are operating out of a hotel room. Their building has entirely burned down. And they didn't have fire protection systems put in.

JA: Aren't they required to?

EY: Sure, every building has to. But it wasn't in.

JA: Was it arson?

EY: Nobody knows. But if you don't have the sprinklers or a fire extinguisher system, the place will burn. Still, isn't it amazing that the biggest computer company in Taiwan burns down, burns for two days, and the fire department couldn't do anything about it? This is the kind of thing that makes you say, "God, can't anyone do anything?" Basically I, myself, like Taiwan, because I was brought up in Taipei and love the place. But eventually they started saying if you criticize a place you don't love it.

JA: Love it or leave it.

EY: Right. So I've just gone along doing my own things and try to do the things I believe in. And not to say much.

JA: Did you get much attention from the fact that so many people, especially critics, and especially critics in the United States, rated *Yi Yi* so highly? Did that get any attention in Taiwan?

EY: Yes, it did. But basically, I don't think the media in general thought that was anything [laughs]. I don't think the media think people there would be interested in news like that [laughs again].

JA: But you'd think that in terms of the world, Taiwan has several world-class filmmakers, and no one pays attention to them? That isn't a story?

EY: Apparently not. [Yang takes a cell-phone call from home and talks with his infant son.]

JA: When you Taiwanese New Wave filmmakers were young, I think you told me, there was one house where you all met?

EY: That was my house. No lock on the door because there was nothing to steal. That was my place.

JA: Were things fermenting there? Did you talk about film? Did you make plans?

EY: Yeah, yeah, but we did a lot of things. If we needed to have a meeting, about subsidy programs or whatever, everyone would show up. The government . . . we were headaches to them.

JA: You told me the story about the coffee guy [laughter]. But is it right that you and Hou Hsiao-hsien don't talk to each other now?

EY: I wouldn't say that, but basically I represent something totally opposite from what his supporters want to do.

JA: Meaning? . . . Sorry.

EY: That's all right. I *can* talk about it. I wouldn't want to.

JA: What about your output? It hasn't been what you would call prolific.

EY: No. Between *The Terrorizer* and *A Brighter Summer Day* was five years, so that's pretty dramatic. Five years. More dramatic, even, because that's when Taiwan politically liberalized. But at the same time a lot of things turned very much like they were in the past. The government was a totalitarian government; you weren't supposed to do a lot of things. But we were confident we were going to change things. But when liberalization happened, our feelings went the opposite way.

JA: What's the feeling with the blockade, U.S.–China [George W. Bush had threatened a blockade of the Strait of Taiwan because of threats from China].

EY: I have very, very terrible feelings about it. It's almost like the fifties, when I was a kid and you had Eisenhower and Nixon and these guys saying Taiwan is the official government of China—"We control the Strait"—and they make you feel America's behind you all the way. Suddenly, there's Ping-Pong diplomacy. Nowadays I almost feel exactly as I did when I was a kid.

Nowadays, it's not that I trust the Chinese government any better than yesterday, but basically I think it helps China to develop its economy. As far as I know, I think the Chinese are good business people; they have good business sense. You don't want people to suffer the fallout like people in the Middle East. If something happened between China and the United States, it's not good for anybody. I think China will liberalize. The leadership—you have to understand the Chinese world . . .

JA: Which no one in the West does.

EY: No, but the leadership, they need to be handled. Give the hardliners some excuse, provide them with some excuse . . .

JA: You have to give them an out.

EY: Right. So basically, I don't think China is going to go back to the Maoist philosophy. Just like Taiwan, they will evolve.

JA: You're a person who makes movies that are about real things, set in a real world. Are you going to approach this situation via film?

EY: Now?

JA: I know you wouldn't approach it head on, but . . .

EY: Right now, I don't have any such plans. I have quite a number of projects that have been in my head for quite a long time. And now I have the resources to do them. So I'll do those first. As far as the present situation, honestly, it doesn't interest me that much, because I know the situation will change. Maybe five years ago, when I was doing *Mahjong*, I very much felt that the present-day situation was very important to me and also I felt it was important to the society. But I was really disappointed because nobody in the place I care so much about paid any attention. I said "Okay."

JA: That seemed to be a movie very specifically about Taipei but which also said something about the general worldview of the nineties.

EY: Yes, all about the time, the media, or information, or disinformation, how it all plays such a role in everyone's life without everyone noticing it. That was the main content of that movie, how we saw the world at that time.

JA: It's a great movie about rationalization, how people skew reality to fit their needs.

EY: Yeah. That's true. But now I have a bunch of projects I really want to do. They might not be that detached from reality, but basically the present situations around the world are simply not that interesting to spend my life examining.

JA: You're waiting for the other shoe to drop.

EY: [Laughs.]

JA: You're not onto anything yet?

EY: Yes, actually, right now I'm working on some of them. Right now, I'm in a better position to do anything I like.

JA: Because of *Yi Yi?*

EY: Yes, and also because the business has changed. Quite a bit, the last few years, especially since the success of last year's films. I think there are some smarter people who begin to see the possibilities. Film is film, still, but it's a locomotive; it drives a lot of other things. And these guys can see it. Right now I think the situation is quite optimistic.

JA: You doing any theater work?

EY: I only do that for fun. No time for fun for the time being.

JA: Was Winstar [the distributor, now Wellspring] pretty cool on *Yi Yi?*

EY: Yes, the film did better than they expected.

JA: And after Cannes this year?

EY: I'm going back, to see my little boy. Sean. Very Irish. His middle name is Shannon. We actually named him Shannon, kind of a neutral name, not knowing whether he was a boy or a girl. But then my family, brother, sister, parents, started saying, "Shannon is for girls." But my wife made a record, wrote a song for the baby and named the song "Shannon." So I said, okay, we'll name the baby Shannon.

JA: One thing I never really talked about with you, which seems odd now, is the American influence on your work—not via rock 'n' roll or comic books, but more sociologically. It seems to me that Taiwan and the United States share a kind of rootlessness, a lack of ethnic unity, that is both a handicap and a blessing. I hear echoes of it in your movies all the time.

EY: This is actually a huge question to ask, and a very simple one to answer. Though the answer may be long, the answers are actually everywhere you look, if you are not as ignorant as most others.

Just yesterday, on CNN, a correspondent filed a simple report, first on violent protests for the Taliban in Islamabad of radical Islamic followers fighting with the police and many were hurt. Then [in] the second part it cut to a rock concert across town that took place the same time as the riots. And it was attended by tens of thousands of Pakistani youth, with their traditional headgear and all. The concert was held by moderate Muslims in support of the international action against the terrorists and Taliban.

The first question I had in my head was: How come no Western media has shown me this before? From the joyful faces of those urban-looking youth still wrapped behind traditional headgear over the girls' heads (perhaps a trendy and fashionable gear for them to exhibit nowadays) you know they have more schooling, more education; are more knowledgeable, more informed, and perhaps they were all on the Web chatting with youth in other parts of the world, and most of all, they show confidence. Whereas the zealous others in the riots look much more desperate.

There is absolutely no need to take sides between the two, for me and for anyone who is not in their shoes. But, if you ask me what was the most telling difference between two entirely opposite groups of the same population, I would definitely tell you the most clear sign of the two: one is not willing to exchange ideas with you, and the other one is!

When someone chooses to be a fanatic, there is a reason and there is a decisionmaking process inside of him or her. And that lack of reason shows in their faces, especially at desperate moments. It has nothing to do with whether he or she is too Americanized, ate too many hamburgers, or is ethnically purified. It has everything to do with what the person knows and thus his or her decision for him- or herself based on such is pretty much decided. Are these moderate youth real Muslims? What's the difference? Do they hate people who don't share their faith? I don't think so! They look as confident as I am about my own faith, and they would do to me exactly what I would do to them: respect their choices of life *after* receiving knowledge of the options we have and [have] made our own choices! This is what we call exchange. This has nothing to do with whether these girls eat at McDonald's and have their coffee at Starbucks. If they choose to, I certainly would respect their choice and not label them as corrupted by Western values, the same way I would look at the radical-minded youth on the other side of town and would not label them as terrorists.

Then, what is the problem? I believe the problem is about those small numbers of people who stood in the middle of this simple divide and took advantage of this polarized situation.

How come I was always told that Arab Muslims were all backward illiterates? How come the films I saw were all about poverty and unfortunate children living in the holes in the hills? How come we were not given the opportunities to sit in discussions, maybe on CNN or other pop media, to review the ideas of the two sides and be more knowledgeable of the situation? Immediately, I knew I had not been told the whole truth all this time, just like those Chinese and Taiwanese films gave Westerners the partial ideas that we were supposed to be miserable and backward, which can only be justified by the word: "ethnicity" or "cultural preferences." These words seem to relate more towards one other simpler word: racism, and nothing else.

What we strive for should be ethnic harmony through these valuable exchanges, instead of ethnic unity. It is clearly impossible and unnecessary to demand ethnic unity, just like you can't demand African Americans to bleach their skin to superficially look similar to you as the only way to bridge racial differences! Part of the reason you thought ethnic unity was the aim was because you have only the superficial, irresponsible view of the situation. And, we are not tropical fish in the ocean that rely on the coral reefs for the entire species to survive! We are not wild mountain dogs in the back desert of Australia, who depend on the environment to be protected from being extinct. What was the difference? The difference I believe is that: we humans go for things! We have our options to take actions, to explore our own destinies and means to survive better! Humans have migrated from [the] deep south of Africa, traveling tens of thousands of miles through hundreds of thousands of years just for that purpose! It was through this process [that] our skin turned from dark to pale as we moved north to self-adjust to the climate and environment while doing so. Other animals instinctively did the similar [thing], but their natural instincts in sociological abilities were just too far behind humans' so their achievements were much less significant. Archaeological evidences have strongly and sufficiently indicated these processes. We gain knowledge as we move along; we share the knowledge to tell others how the world is and how nature works so that we ultimately could bring better lives and improvements of human conditions to all people on this planet indiscriminately!

Of course, there are always those who don't have the courage to come along; they don't have the courage or confidence to even be curious enough to enjoy new knowledge that requires courage and optimism to discover. Ironically, with their minds in the dark, they are more desperate to receive authoritative words to shine a light on their shivering and fragile souls. They have to make [a] tremendous amount of assumptions of how nature must be, with their limited knowledge during the process, to knit together a logical explanation they call philosophy, to demand the masses to follow. Because of this complex fear of being recognized as inferior, triggered by the lack of total knowledge and the unproven wishful assumptions that fill the holes of these teachings, their subconscious intolerance of people who do not go along is much more severe and sensitive!

Confucianism was done this way: It pretended to be the ultimate answer for eternity, and, of course, this now seems ridiculously impossible! Christianity did the same, so those conscientious scientists looking for truth got burned to death as witches! So, do we see a pattern now for the World Trade Center tragedy? Yes, we do. Of course, we do. How can that be overlooked?

So, this is where "the crack" always sits.

Knowledge is about truth! Truth has no boundary. So, between those extremist Muslims who riot with the police and the youth moderates enjoying the rock concert, what was the difference that made them either interact with you or not? Unfortunately[,] the answer is quite simple: knowledge. This is the danger when democracy turns into a tyranny for the majority, which in turn is manipulated by only a very few. If illiterates act a certain way, it most likely cannot meet with our agreement because of their lack of references to base their judgments on. If we say we have to respect their judgments because we have to respect their ethnicity, then there is a huge inconsistency and a huge bias of irresponsibility here that is simply called prejudice.

Science and arts are not ethnical; they should be the most universal. They belong to not just humans categorized by race, but belong to life and life alone! Culture evolves, just like life itself. How can culture be segregated unless you in your mind have decided that humans should be segregated [and] thus cultures can be purified, like Hitler and Himmler once tried seventy years ago! Do we really have to go into that again and again? If we don't learn from history, what does it mean by evolution? Wasn't evolution the exact alibi Hitler used in his attempt to purify his race?

It is prejudice to think that intelligence belongs only to things ethnic or local and not universal. It is racism to simplemindedly think that anyone knowledgeable enough to [understand that] foreign [influences are] corrupt or commercialized or globalized must not know anything about his or her own culture[,] or [that he or she is] too corrupt to even identify with his or her own culture. Hand in hand, very often, this usually Western mentality becomes automatically a haven for those who play only to these prejudiced Westerners hiding behind their own ethnicity[,] because they know for certain that these Westerners who support them are ignorant of their ethnicity and incapable of telling that they are exploiting the situation. So, "the crack" is now being exploited for [a] vast amount of advantages to the small number of manipulators.

So, I was called Americanized, westernized, traitor, or "bananas" by people who have [a stake in] exploiting this "crack" so they can hide behind this ethnic black box, because they feel threatened that I always raise questions that challenge their monopoly on our cultural future. My criticism of my own culture has nothing to do with my knowledge of Western culture or how much I agree with it. When our own culture has big holes in it, I'll try my best to mend it[,] and it is my duty, just as it was for those scientists taken as witches who got burned alive five hundred years ago in Europe. Those who try to burn me alive hide exactly behind this "ethnic unity" façade, which only ignorant and irresponsible outsiders [are] incline[d] to think exists, because most of the time these outsiders don't care to tell [the difference] between things backward or ethnic, either way.

I feel very fortunate that I was born in a cosmopolitan town like Shanghai, with parents from the most diverse and opposite polarities of the faceless middle population of China, and raised in a town like Taipei, which was quite international for that period of history. I got a chance to see all kinds of different people from all over China, and from all over the world. I did what I enjoyed doing from the time I was very young. Before I even turned ten, I secretly helped myself to loads of classical Chinese literature without telling my father, just to explore my own fantasy world of creating manga stories. I did classic calligraphy other kids never had a chance to even touch. I was inspired early and went into classical drawing and painting so young that my friends thought I was weird. Just as [with] the various kinds of movies from all the different countries, I was exposed to all kinds of dialects and languages, Japanese, English, French, even some German, which one of the Catholic priests who used to visit our school taught us. I have traveled the world, and never once have I had the experience of not being able to understand certain people's situations when I ran into them. I asked questions and got answers for myself to study and make judgments, and all of the time they all make perfect human sense[,] and never for once did I think something was beyond my comprehension, that I had to categorize it in some ethnic black box, because I knew I cared, and therefore I got answers, my own answers.

If you are too lazy to bother and just throw this intricate issue into a pile that's roughly labeled "ethnicity," of course, this "I-couldn't-care-less" mentality won't get you anywhere except an easy excuse of "respect" for something you don't know and which is actually something you don't care to know.

So it works both ways, because there are those who don't care to know and just hide behind the easy excuse of "respecting others' ethnicity" to disguise their lack of interest. Or, on the other side, there are those who play to this disguise by building a wall of ethnicity that explains away everything that others don't understand as something ethnical so that they can receive "respect" from these foreigners by hiding their incompetence and lack of effort behind these façades of ethnicity built right next to the crack.

Taiwan basically is very similar to America. About the same time the pilgrims set sail from Britain to North America, mainland Chinese did the same to Taiwan. Taiwan has always been an immigrant society populated with people who moved outward and tried their luck in a new land instead of staying with the old rules and social orders. So, we can either say Taiwan is very much like America or we can say the reverse:

America is much like Taiwan, though few would make the reversion, since Taiwan is so much smaller.

We don't have to set sails to North America or Taiwan anymore nowadays. Humans have invented films, airplanes, electronic communication, digital technology, et cetera. Our presence, physical or otherwise, can move around the world in a matter of seconds, not months and years. Any barriers we tried to pretend there have been are simply symbolic at best and remain mostly pacifiers to those who have difficulty in receiving and comprehending new knowledge. So, to this day in human history, there should be no un-understandable knowledge that we call "ethnic" any more, unless there is a deliberate attempt to *not* make oneself understood by camouflaging this antagonism inside a dark bottle which it demands you to "respect." Respect we do, but unfortunately, sometimes this respect for things ethnic falls right into the trap of some folks' alibi of not being capable of understanding the essence of the diversity, which requires knowledge and ability to make sense of it all. This falls right into the laps of those who play the ethnicity card to receive praise for their lack of capability to understand, lack of capability to interact, and, worst of all, lack of capability to care.

So, the world has clearly come to a point where it is divided by a visible line: on the one side there are those who enjoy knowledge and on the other, those who fear knowledge. When they enjoy knowledge, they are all ready to exchange for more and make life more meaningful day by day. When they fear knowledge, they must resort to things radical to balance the unbalanceable.

Unfortunately, of the groups that fear knowledge, a massive majority are actually victims deprived of knowledge and education by this very small number of people who are exploiting this crack. This same small number of people finds all kinds of ways to mislead the world by grouping the conscientious few with the worst exploiters: big businesses, especially and mostly American business. So, we love films, because films bring all different kinds of people together with a universal language. But, what do they do after anti-American protests besides burning down McDonald's and Starbucks? They burn down movie theaters, since films have long been labeled the same: American influence.

Not unlike Pakistan, every country is actually now in the same situation, divided right in the middle by this clear line of division, including both America and Taiwan! Look at those guys in the Midwest attending World Series games as compared to those at Yankee Stadium. Look at those states that went cleanly for George W. Bush and those that went cleanly for Al Gore. And, look at those rifle association members and those who decided to bomb federal buildings. Are they ready to exchange ideas with you? Sometimes I really have doubts. I was fortunate to have the chance to really get to know some of the real rednecks when I was going to school in Florida. This is when I am most confident to say that we are all similar and the only difference is how we know and what we know! After exchanges, we became close friends. One of my friend's father actually even became one of the first American businessmen who ventured to Taiwan to take part in the early seventies Taiwan's export boom.

The enjoyment of having more knowledge is not "American influence." It's not even called influence either. It's called inspiration, human inspiration. Like everyone else, America is part of it, not that it is only part of America. You can't say someone is part of it like America and you go label the guy Americanized. To enjoy knowing more is simply the process of enjoying life and what life offers. It's a simple process to root oneself in the deep soil of this planet Earth, which should no longer be segregated by the artificial borders we once drew in the backward histories centuries ago! There are many like me in New York, or San Francisco, or Seattle, or Gainesville, Florida; there are also many more in Tokyo, Shanghai, Hong Kong, Seoul, Singapore, Paris, Berlin, London, and, now I know, Islamabad and what have you. We are not Americanized; before we are anything, we are just human beings living in the twenty-first century. We have open arms, to receive as well as to give.

The Winter of 1905 (1905 Nian De Dongtian), 1981
Taiwan
Feature film for television
Direction: Yu Weizheng
Executive producer: Yu Weiyan, Zhan Hongzhi
Screenplay: Edward Yang
Cinematography: Kim Tokusho, Lai Fengyan
Sound: Du Duzhhi
Editing: Chen Bowen
Cast: Wang Xiajun, Qin Zhimin, Tsui Hark
Color
110 minutes

Expectations (Zhiwang), 1984
Taiwan
Episode 2 of four-episode feature film, *In Our Time*
Production: Central Motion Picture Corporation (CMPC), Taiwan
Distribution: CMPC
Direction: Edward Yang
Executive producer: Ming Ji
Producer: Xu Guoliang
Project coordinator: Zhao Qibin
Screenplay: Edward Yang
Cinematography: Chen Jiamo
Sound: Du Duzhi
Editing: Liao Qingsong
Cast: Shi Anni, Zhang Yingzhen, Wang Qiguang
Color
30 minutes

That Day, on the Beach (*Haitan De Yitian*), 1983
Hong Kong/Taiwan
Feature film
Production: Cinema City Corp., Hong Kong; CMPC, Taipei
Distribution: Cinema City Corp., Hong Kong; CMPC, Taipei
Direction: Edward Yang
Executive producers: Ming Ji, Wang Yingxiang, Mak Ga
Associate producers: Xu Guoliang, Sek Tin, Zhao Qibin, Wong Bak Ming
Production supervisors: Sylvia Chang, Xiao Ye, Yu Kanping, Duan Zhongyi
Screenplay: Edward Yang, Wu Nianzhen
Cinematography: Christopher Doyle, Zhang Huigong
Sound: Du Duzhi
Editing: Liao Qingsong
Music: Lin Minyi
Cast: Sylvia Chang, Terry Hu, Steven Hsu, David Mao, Li Lie
Color
166 minutes

Taipei Story (*Qingmei Zhuma*), 1985
Taiwan
Feature film
Production: Evergreen Films
Distribution: Jane Balfour Films, London
Direction: Edward Yang
Executive Producers: Lin Rongfeng, Hou Hsiao-hsein
Producers: Huang Yong, Liu Shenzhong
Screenplay: Edward Yang, Hou Hsiao-hsien, Zhu Tian-wen
Cinematography: Yang Weihan
Editing: Wang Jiyang, Song Fanzhen
Cast: Tsai Chin, Hou Hsiao-hsien, Wu Nianzhen
Color
110 minutes

The Terrorizer (*Kongbu Fenzi*), 1986
Taiwan/Hong Kong
Feature film
Production: Golden Harvest, Hong Kong; Sunny Overseas Corp., Taipei
Distribution: Jane Balfour Films
Direction: Edward Yang
Executive producers: Raymond Chow, Lin Dengfei
Associate producer: Xy Guoliang
Project coordinator: Zhao Qibin
Screenplay: Edward Yang, Xiao Ye
Cinematography: Zhang Zhan, Zheng Fuxing

Sound: Du Duzhi
Editing: Liao Qingsong
Art direction: Lai Mingtang
Music: Edward Yang, Ong Xiaoliang
Cast: Cora Miao, Li Liqun, Wang An, Jin Shijie
Color
109 minutes

A Brighter Summer Day (Gulingjie Shaonian Sharen Shijian), 1991
Taiwan
Feature film
Production: Yang and His Gang Filmmakers
Distribution: Jane Balfour Films, London
Direction: Edward Yang
Executive producers: Edward Yang, Stan Lai, Lin Xingnan, Zheng Shuizhi
Producers: Zhan Hongzhi, Jiang Fenqi
Associate producer: Yu Weiyan
Screenplay: Edward Yang
Cinematography: Zhang Huigong, Li Longyu
Sound: Du Duzhi
Editing: Chen Bowen
Art direction: Yu Weiyan
Music: Edward Yang
Cast: Lisa Yang, Zhang Zhen, Zhang Guozhu, Elaine Jin
Color
237 minutes

A Confucian Confusion (Duli Shidai), 1994
Taiwan
Feature film
Production: AtomFilms and Theater
Distribution: AtomFilms and Theater
Direction: Edward Yang
Executive producer: David Sun
Associate producer: Yu Weiyan
Screenplay: Edward Yang
Cinematography: Arthur Wong, Zhang Zhan, Li Longyu, Hong Wuxiu
Sound: Du Duzhi
Editing: Chen Bowen
Music: Antonio Lee
Cast: Chen Xiangqi, Ni Shujun, David Wang, Wang Bosen, Richie Li, Danny
    Deng, Wang Yeming
Color
125 minutes

Mahjong (Majiang), 1996
Taiwan
Feature film
Production: AtomFilms and Theater
Distribution: AtomFilms and Theater
Direction: Edward Yang
Executive producer: Edward Yang
Associate producer: Yu Weiyan
Screenplay: Edward Yang
Cinematography: Li Yixu, Li Longyu
Sound: Du Duzhi
Editing: Chen Bowen
Music: Forward Records
Cast: Virginie Ledoyen, Tang Congsheng, Ke Yuluen, Zhang Zhen, Wang Qizan, Carrie Ng
Color
121 minutes

Yi Yi (A One and a Two . . .), 2000
Taiwan/Japan
Feature film
Production: AtomFilms and Theater
Distribution: WinStar
Direction: Edward Yang
Executive producers: Shina Kawai, Naoko Tsukeda
Associate producers: Yu Weiyen, Osamu Kubota
Screenplay: Edward Yang
Cinematography: Yang Weihan, Li Longyu
Sound: Du Duzhi
Editing: Chen Bowen
Music: Kaili Peng
Cast: Wu Nianzhen, Elaine Jin, Kelly Lee, Jonathan Chang, Issy Ogata
Color
173 minutes

Miluku Family (Niunaitang Jiating), 2001–4
Taiwan
Ongoing animation series that includes:
   Lovers' Way (Qingren Zhilu)
   Lotto Craze (Letouyou)
   Miluku Family (Niunaitang Jiating)
   Taipei Chic (Taibei Nusheng)
   !r-Rational Theatre (!Guojiajuyuan)

Celebrities Recommend (*Mingren Tuijian*)
The Jogger (*Chenpao Gungyuan*)
He Sings (*Tantang Qingeji*)
Production: Kailidoscope, Inc.
Direction: Edward Yang
Executive producer: Kaili Peng
Stories: Edward Yang
Character design: Edward Yang
Art direction: Edward Yang
Sound: Du Duzhi
Animation: Kailidoscope Studio

Andrews, Nigel. "The Perfect Midlife Crisis: *A One and a Two* Is the Best Film of the Year and Probably the Best Film of the Decade." *Financial Times* (London), edition 1, Apr. 5, 2001, http://specials.ft.com (accessed Oct. 2004).

Arnold, William. "Former Seattle Resident Earns Acclaim as Director." *Seattle Post-Intelligencer*, Jan. 18, 2001, http://seattlepi.nwsource.com (accessed Oct. 2004).

Babcock, William A. "Edward Yang Gives Taiwan Direction." *Christian Science Monitor*, north sports, final edition, Dec. 15, 1988.

Carr, Jay. "Taiwan's *Yi Yi* Gets Nod from Society of Film Critics." *Boston Globe*, Jan. 8, 2001.

Chen, Leo Chanjen. "A Frustrated Architect." *New Left Review*, Sept.–Oct. 2001, www.newleftreview.net (accessed Oct. 2004).

Darcy, David, reporter, and Bob Edwards, anchor. "Edward Yang, Taiwanese Director." *Morning Edition,* NPR, Nov. 1, 2000, http://www.npr.org/templates/story/story.php?storyId=1113289 (accessed Oct. 2004).

Dargis, Manohla. "Life and Death and Everything Else in Edward Yang's *Yi Yi.*" *L.A. Weekly*, Dec. 1–7, 2000, http://www.laweekly.com/ink/01/02/film-dargis.php (accessed Oct. 2004).

Jaffer, Mehru. "Asian Filmmakers Say Long Arm of the Censor Still a Problem." *Jakarta Post,* Apr. 21, 2001.

Jameson, Fredric. "Remapping Taipei." In *The Geopolitical Aesthetic: Cinema and Space in the World System.* Bloomington: Indiana University Press, 1992. 114–57.

Janusonis, Michael. "Who Is Edward Yang? Find Out This Weekend." *Providence Journal-Bulletin*, Mar. 1, 1996.

Johnston, Sheila. "Talk of the Global Village." *Times* (London), Apr. 5, 2001.

King, Loren. "Programmed to Direct: *Yi Yi* Filmmaker Edward Yang Favors His High-Tech Past with Humanity." *Chicago Tribune*, Chicagoland final edition, Feb. 11, 2001.

Kraicer, Shelly, and Lisa Roosen-Runge. "Edward Yang: A Taiwanese Independent Filmmaker in Conversation." *CineAction* 47, special edition, "Anything

But Hollywood," Oct. 1998, 48–55, http://www.chinesecinemas.org/yang. html.

Leonard, John. Review of *Yi Yi*. *CBS Sunday Morning*, Oct. 8, 2000.

Malcolm, Derek. "A One and a Two: Spare Portrait of Urban Living Is Yang's Best Yet." *Screen International*, Cannes, May 17, 2000.

Mirsky, Jonathan. "Inside the Whale." *New York Review of Books*, Dec. 20, 2001.

Nabokov, Vladimir. *Lectures on Literature*. New York: Harcourt, Brace, Jovanovich, 1980.

Ou, Alice, ed. *Taiwan Films*. Taipei: Variety Publishing Co., 1993.

Rosenbaum, Jonathan. "Exiles in Modernity: The Films of Edward Yang." *Chicago Reader*, http://www.chireader.com/movies/archives/1197/11077.htm (accessed Oct. 2004).

Sklar, Robert. *A World History of Film*. New York: Abrams, 2002.

Winfrey, Yayoi Lena. "Edward Yang Talks Best through His Films." *Northwest Asian Weekly*, Ethnic NewsWatch, Jan. 19, 2001.

Yang, Edward. Interview by John Anderson, Cannes, May 2000.

———. Interview by John Anderson, Cannes, May 2001.

———. Interview by John Anderson, ongoing via e-mail, 2001–3.

———. "Taiwan Stories." Interview by Leo Chanjen Chen. *New Left Review*, Sept.–Oct. 2001, www.newleftreview.net (accessed Oct. 2004).

Page numbers in italics denote photographs

Academy Awards, 85
Aguirre, the Wrath of God (film), 6
AIDS, 68
Allen, Woody, 2
American Bandstand (TV show), 61
American influences: in *A Brighter Summer Day*, 59; in *Mahjong*, 82; in Yang's work generally, 100
American Pie 2 (film), 85
Andrews, Nigel, 10
"Angel Baby" (song), 61
Antonioni, Michelangelo, 3, 77, 87
"Aquarius" (song), 82
Asthenic Syndrome, The (film), 56
Atom Films and Theater, 10
Auden, W. H., 1

Baez, Joan, 104
Beijing Film Academy, 12
Beatles, The, 23, 24
Beautiful Duckling (film), 13
Beckett, Samuel, 87
Bergman, Ingmar, 102
Bergman, Ingrid, 102
Blue Angel, The (film), 63
Bonnes Femmes, Les (film), 30
Borrowed Life, A (film), 13, 85
Brighter Summer Day, A (film), 4, 5, 11, 14, 16–21, 25, 27, 54–65, 77, 80, 93; Americanisms in, 59; conformity and change in, 64; feminism in, 18; gen-

erational conflict in, 57–58; Japanese influences in, 62; preparation for, 56; theme of unity in, 15
Broadway Boogie-Woogie (painting), 38
Buddha Bless America (film), 85
Burroughs, William S., 9
Bush, George W., 107, 116

Cannes Film Festival, 4, 98
Carey, Mariah, 66, 75
Carter, Jimmy, 6
CBS Sunday Morning (TV show), 85
Central Film Bureau, 12
Central Motion Picture Bureau, 12
Central Motion Picture Corporation, 21, 97
Chabrol, Claude, 2, 30, 80
Chang, Grace, 16
Chang, Jonathan, 85, 98
Chang, Sylvia, 29, 33
Chang Yi, 21
Change Is a Revolving Wheel (book), 52
Chanjen Chin, Leo, 44
Cheever, John, 3
Chen Kaige, 12
Chen Yiwen, 76
Chiang Kai-shek, 14, 17, 80, 84, 101
Chiao, Peggy, 51
Chiung Yao, 13
Chou Yu-fen, 52
Christianity, 112
Citizen Kane (film), 10, 26, 54, 105
City of Sadness (film), 14, 56
Close-up (film), 56

Confucian Confusion, A (film), 4, 5,
    66–77; and Asian economic boom, 67;
    corruption of culture portrayed in, 68;
    and "emotional factor," 69; ethics in,
    72; meaning of sincerity in, 68
Confucianism, 66, 76, 112
Confucius, 66, 68, 69, 84
Cool Hand Luke (film), 48
corporate narrative, 17
Crouching Tiger, Hidden Dragon (film),
    85, 99, 105
Cultural Revolution, 12

Dargis, Manohla, 74
Dean, James, 64
"desolate negative epiphany," 44
Disneyland, 59
Dr. Doolittle 2 (film), 85
Dupuis, Diana, 78
Dust in the Wind (film), 85
Dylan, Bob, 104

Eisenhower, Dwight D., 107
Eisenstein, Sergei, 47
EMI, 66
Ephron, Nora, 84
Erickson, Nick, 78
Escape from Fort Bravo (film), 8
Expectations (film), 4, 14, 20–25; mobility
    as metaphor in, 24

Fassbinder, Rainer Werner, 6
Faulkner, William, 30
Fitzcarraldo (film), 6
Fitzgerald, F. Scott, 44
Floating Weeds (film), 7
Ford, John, 56
Four Loves (film), 13

Gates, Bill, 88
General Electric, 17
Gillespie, Dizzy, 9
Glitter (film), 66
Golden Harvest, 12
Good Men, Good Women (film), 56
Gore, Al, 115
Grand Motion Picture Company, 13
Great Gatsby, The (novel), 44

Green Plum and Bamboo Stalk (film,
    poem), 37
Gu Baoming, 82

Hamsun, Knute, 68
Harry Potter and the Sorcerer's Stone
    (film), 84
Hawthorne, Nathaniel, 9
"healthy realism," 12, 21
Hemingway, Ernest, 22
Herzog, Werner, 6, 7
Himmler, Heinrich, 112
Hitchcock, Alfred, 80
Hitler, Adolf, 113
Holden, William, 8
Hong Kong cinema, 11, 12
Hou Hsiao-hsien, 9, 13, 14, 15, 16, 36,
    41, 85, 107
Hou Tsai Chin, 39
Hu, Terry, 29
Huang Chun-ming, 13
Hui, Ann, 85

In Our Time (film), 4, 21
In the Mood for Love (film), 99
Irish literature, 11
Italian Neo-Realism, 3, 4

Jameson, Fredric, 46
Jannings, Emil, 63
Jin, Elaine, 93
Joyce, James, 2, 87

Ke Suyun, 86
Ke Yizheng, 36
Ke Yuluen, 83
Keaton, Buster, 86
Kehr, Dave, 21
Kerouac, Jack, 9
Kiarostami, Abbas, 56
Kinski, Klaus, 6
Kitano, Takeshi, 49
Ko I-cheng
Kulishev, Lev, 47
Kulishev effect, 47

Lai, Stan, 16
Ledoyen, Virginie, 78, 92

Lee, Bruce, 12
Lee, Kelly, 85, 98
Leonard, John, 3, 85
Li Ang, 18
Li Bo, 37
Li Han-hsiang, 13
Li Liqun, 53
Li Xing, 13
Life and Nothing More (film), 56
Light from Last Night, The (film), 13
Lime, Harry, 62
Little League World Series, 43, 44
Locarno Film Festival, 34
Lumumba (film), 84

Machiavelli, 70
Mahjong (film), 4, 5, 11, 18, 77–84, 92
Mamet, David, 74
manga, 51
Mao, David, 33
Mao Zedong, 5, 14, 84
McDonald's, 92, 101, 110, 115
Melville, Herman, 9
Miao, Cora, *49, 53*
Mickey Mouse, 59
Mondrian, Piet, 38
Monroe, Marilyn, 44
montage theory, 47

National Society of Film Critics, 84
NBA, 75, 76
Nelson, Ricky, 63
New Left Review, 6
New York Film Critics Circle, 84
Nixon, Richard, 107
Nosferatu (film), 6

October Revolution, 47
Of Human Bondage (film), 63
Ozu, 37

Panic (film), 84
Parker, Charlie, 9
Peng Kaili, 89
Presley, Elvis, 29, 61, 65
Proust, Marcel, 30
Puppetmaster, The (film), 56

Ray, Nicholas, 64
Renoir, Jean, 4, 80
Rio Lobo (film), 63
Rosenbaum, Jonathan: on *A Brighter Summer Day*, 56; on *Taipei Story*, 3
Rules of the Game, The (film), 80
Russian State Film School, 47

Sandwich Man, The (film), 13
San Francisco Film Festival, 7
Satantango (film), 56
Scary Movie 2 (film), 85
September 11, 2001, 15
Shanghai cinema, 11, 12
Shaw Brothers studio, 11
Shi Anni, 22, 23
Shu Qi, 96
"Smoke Gets in Your Eyes" (song), 50
socialist realism, 12
Sontag, Susan, 91
Starbucks, 110, 115
Strawman, The (film), 14
Strike (film), 47
"Sukiyaki" (song), 89
Sun Yadong, *26*

Taipei, institutional obsolescence in, 51
Taipei Story (film), 4, 5, 9, 11, 17, 18, 31, 34–44, 57, 77, 80
Taiwan: audiences in, 4; business corruption in, 11, 39; character of, 5; censorship in, 7; conformity in, 30, 64, 77, 95; "February 28 incident," 11, 14; flight to, 54; and KMT (Kuomintang), 6, 11; martial law in, 7; and materialism, 5; and Nationalists, 5, 14, 20; and national narrative, 17; population of, 10; size of, 10, westernization of, 13. *See also* Taipei; Taiwanese cinema; Taiwanese literature; Taiwanese media; Taiwanese New Wave
Taiwanese cinema, 1, 13, 95–98
Taiwanese literature: modernists in, 13; nativists in, 13
Taiwanese media, 102
Taiwanese New Wave, 2, 4, 6, 8, p.8, 13, 15, 96, 102, 107
Taliban, 110

Tang Congsheng, 82, 83
Tang Ruyun, 86
Tao, Michael, 86
Tao Te-chen, 21
Tarr, Bela, 56
Taste of Cherry (film), 56
Terrorizer, The (film), 2, 4, 5, 17, 18, 45–53, 55; montage theory in, 47, 48. *See also* White Chick
That Day, on the Beach (film), 3–5, 18–20, 26–34, 38, 77, 80, 85
Third Man, The (film), 62
Tiananmen Square, 11
Time to Live and a Time to Die, A (film), 9
Tokyo Story (film), 37
Tolstoy, Leo, 5
Tsai Chin, 36, 41
Tsai Ming-liang, 16
Turgenev, Ivan, 22

Ulysses (novel), 87, 88
United Nations, 6
University of Florida, 6
University of Southern California, 6

Variety, 84
Vermeer, Jan, 2
Vertov, Dziga, 47
Vietnam War, 24

Wang Bosen, 72, 83
Wang Qiguang, 23
Wang Tong, 14
Wang Yeming, 76
War and Peace (novel), 62
Welles, Orson, 26
West Side Story (musical), 54
White Chick, 45, 48–50, 52
Winter of 1905, The (film), 7
Wong Kar-wai, 98
Wu Nianzhen, 9, 13, 85

Xiao Shushen, 86
Xu Shuyuan, 89

Yang and His Gang, 10
Yang, Edward, 98; birth and background of, 100; and computers, 6; and decision to enter filmmaking, 6; and engineering, 88, 96; and manga, 114
—filmwork themes of: corporate narrative, 17; doorways, 79, 91; dualities, 28, 59, 85, 92; home as symbol, 29; patriarch as fraud, 80; reflections, 91; subordinate characters, 27, 43, 80; "transcendent moments," 31, 44, 64, 74–75, 88; "urban trilogy," 5
—personal perspectives of: on architecture, 35, 38, 44; on being a "good Chinese son," 6; on fate, 45; on fathers, 80; on fiction, 46, 50, 53; on gender issues, 18, 31, 32, 35, 40; on Hollywood, 9; on innocence, 70; on life versus art, 74; on money, 70; on mothers, 18, 93; on nonactors, 96; on own work, 4, 10, 108, 113; on racism, 111; on religion, 92–93, 110; on sincerity; 68; on solitude, 94; on struggle and art, 28–29; on Taipei, 34–35, 37, 106; on Taipei morality, 79; on Taiwan media, 106–7; on U.S. distribution, 4, 9, 16; on youth, 42–43, 101–2
Yang, Lisa, 58
Yi Yi (film), 3, 10, 17, 20, 21; inspiration for, 10; 57, 77
Yon Anshuen, 51
Yu Weizeng, 7

Zeng Xinyi, 86
Zhang Yimou, 12
Zhang Yingzhen, 26
Zhang Zhen, 58, 63, 105
Zhang Ziyi, 106

John Anderson is chief film critic for *Newsday*. He also writes for the *Los Angeles Times, L.A. Weekly, Billboard, Washington Post, The Nation,* and other publications. He is the author of *Sundancing: Hanging Out and Listening In at America's Most Important Film Festival.* Anderson served as chair of the New York Film Critics Circle and is a member of the National Society of Film Critics, the critics group FIPRESCI, and the National Book Critics Circle. He is a former member of the New York Film Festival Selection Committee.

Books in the series Contemporary Film Directors

Edward Yang
    John Anderson

Wong Kar-wai
    Peter Brunette

Claire Denis
    Judith Mayne

Joel and Ethan Coen
    R. Barton Palmer

Nelson Pereira dos Santos
    Darlene J. Sadlier

Abbas Kiarostami
    Mehrnaz Saeed-Vafa and Jonathan Rosenbaum

The University of Illinois Press
is a founding member of the
Association of American University Presses.

Composed in 10/13 New Caledonia
with Helvetica Neue display
by Jim Proefrock
at the University of Illinois Press
Designed by Paula Newcomb
Manufactured by Sheridan Books, Inc.

University of Illinois Press
1325 South Oak Street
Champaign, IL 61820-6903
www.press.uillinois.edu